Sullivan's List

THE 100 MOST AMAZING EVENTS IN THE WORLD

INDEX

JUNE

45. **El Colacho** – *Spain*
46. **Stinging Nettle Eating Championship** – *England*
47. **Santo António** – *Portugal*
48. **Bodypaint Festival** – *Austria*
49. **Naked Bike Ride** – *Spain*
50. **Calcio Storico** – *Italy*
51. **Stonehenge** – *England*
52. **San Joan** – *Spain*
53. **Inti Raymi** – *Peru*
54. **Kırkpınar** – *Turkey*

JULY

55. **Gettysburg Civil War Reenactment** – *US*
56. **Il Palio** – *Italy*
57. **Ufo Festival** – *US*
58. **Bous a la Mar** – *Spain*
59. **Eukonkanto** – *Finland*
60. **Running of the Bulls** – *Spain*
61. **Amtrak Mooning** – *US*
62. **Boryeong Mud Festival** – *South Korea*
63. **Mwaka Kogwa** – *Tanzania*
64. **Redneck Games** – *US*
65. **At Chabysh** – *Kyrgyzstan*
66. **Fiesta de la Tirana** – *Chile*
67. **Hemingway Days** – *US*
68. **Festival of the Near-Dead** – *Spain*
69. **Darwin Beer Can Regatta** – *Australia*
70. **Rasta Earth Festival** – *South Africa*

AUGUST

71. **Canal Parade** – *Netherlands*
72. **Fêtes de Bayonne** – *France*
73. **Maralal Camel Derby** – *Kenya*
74. **Medeltidsveckan** – *Sweden*
75. **La Régate des Baignoires** – *Belgium*
76. **Tetsuya Odori** – *Japan*
77. **Henly on Todd Regatta** – *Australia*
78. **Eid al-Fitr** – *Syria*
79. **Bog Snorkeling** – *Wales*
80. **La Tomatina** – *Spain*
81. **Air Guitar Festival** – *Finland*
82. **Cowal Highland Gathering** – *Scotland*
83. **Umhlanga** – *Swaziland*

SEPTEMBER

84. **Burning Man** – *US*
85. **La Muixeranga** – *Spain*
86. **Sukkot** – *Israel*
87. **Art Car** – *US*
88. **Vegetarian Festival** – *Thailand*
89. **Oktoberfest** – *Germany*
90. **Gorilla Run** – *England*

OCTOBER

91. **Les Batailles de Reines** – *Switzerland*
92. **Angola Rodeo** – *US*
93. **Ghadames festival** – *Libya*
94. **Diwali** – *India*
95. **Halloween** – *US*

NOVEMBER

96. **Día del Gaucho** – *Argentina*
97. **Día de los Muertos** – *Mexico*
98. **Loy Krathong** – *Thailand*
99. **Pirates Week** – *Cayman Islands*

DECEMBER

100. **Noche de los Rabanos** – *Mexico*

Introduction

This book is dedicated to all the adventurers who shared their stories, experiences, photos and tips to help create Sullivan's List. Their experiences prove that, every now and then, people all over the world are seeking new ways to break out of their daily rhythms and live life to the fullest. Whether their goal is to quiet the ghosts, to please the gods, or to celebrate the arrival of spring, all of these traditions and events bring people closer together. For that one moment in time, everyone is equal and all problems are forgotten.

Leaf through these pages and explore the many incredible events that make up Sullivan's List. Read, marvel, get inspired, and... pack your bags and go!

We wish you a great journey.

01

New Years Dive

WHAT BETTER WAY TO START THE NEW YEAR WITH A DIP INTO THE ICE COLD NORTH SEA? SOUNDS CRAZY? AT LEAST YOU'LL BE CLEAN, FRESH AND HANGOVER-FREE.

Why would thousands of Dutch people willingly spend their New Year's Day diving into waters that are barely warm enough for swimming even in the summer months? For fun. The tradition has existed only since 1960, when a man with the funny Dutch name of Ok van Batenburg organized a New Year's dip off the beach at Zandvoort for his swimmer friends. Five years later, the event moved to the beach at Scheveningen, near The Hague.

Nearly ten thousand people gather together on the beach at 12 noon. Ready to run, they count down, standing butt cheek by jowl and staring at the cold, uninviting sea. This being Holland, a good portion of the swimmers are clad in orange

hats and bathing suits (if they choose to wear them at all). There are entire families braving the waters together, as well as student groups – beers in hand – still up since the previous evening's celebrations. There are people in long pants, people in weird costumes, fat people in thongs, and pretty girls in bikinis waiting to be discovered by the ever-present members of the media. To warm up after their frosty dip, many swimmers indulge in some strong drinks and pea soup, a Dutch winter delicacy.

The Dutch are not alone in undertaking a New Year's "Polar Bear" swim – similar events take place in many Western countries – but in few places is the occasion celebrated with such

exuberance. In England and America, the events are often linked to charities. You do not plunge for yourself, but to collect money for a good cause. In many non-Western cultures, it's a tradition to bathe on New Year's Day to purify yourself and rid yourself of evil. After a night of heavy drinking, a dash into these icy waters should leave you feeling fresh and ready for the new year.

Festival au Désert 02

DON'T EXPECT ANY SHUTTLE BUSES TO AND FROM THE PARKING LOT. THIS FESTIVAL TAKES PLACE BEYOND TIMBUKTU, LITERALLY, IN THE NORTH OF MALI. PERHAPS THE DIFFICULT TREK OVER THE UNDULATING DUNES, WHICH STAND OUT SO STARKLY AGAINST THE DESERT SKY, IS WHAT MAKES THIS EVENT SO EXCEPTIONAL.

The Festival au Désert is a music festival, but it's also much more than that. The festival was born out of the traditional activities of the Touaregs, the nomadic people of the southern Sahara. The Touaregs have a longstanding tradition of coming together annually for big meetings during which they discuss challenges and conflicts but also reconnect with each other and have a good time. For hours, they will sit chatting on the mats in their tents. Touaregs also play their traditional music during these reunions, and music is, of course, central to the Festival au Désert. The festival was, like the people who inspired it, nomadic in nature for the first few years of its existence (it began in 2001), but it is now held annually in Essakane. Since this is an actual Touareg site, festivalgoers cannot just bring any old tent and pitch it there; it's necessary that the temporary desert city that sprouts up during the festival be as genuine as possible. For, although the festival is increasingly oriented to tourists – to generate money for this poor and unstable region – the organization wants the festival to remain a gathering spot for locals. Ideally, it should be a party for Touaregs, but one which tourists can attend. You can rent a place to sleep like a nomad in one of the white tents, with or without a mattress. There is food available at one of the

 MALI

Essakane, Mali.

 ORIGIN

The first festival was held in 2001, inspired by the traditional Touareg gatherings. At that first event, music was just one of the components, but now the festival features thirty acts from Mali and the rest of the world.

 PARTICIPATE

The organization of the festival makes you, whether you like it or not, more than just a consumer at this festival. The €15 that you pay for a ticket goes to support the local economy.

ESSAKANE

TRAVEL

BAMAKO

It's best not to try to travel out to Essakane on your own. The festival's organizers recommend arranging transportation in advance or, better yet, making use of the buses and jeeps that travel from Timbuktu to the festival.

 TIPS

For more information on the festival, tickets, and sleeping arrangements, visit **www.festival-au-desert.org**.

many restaurants, as well as toilets which are, especially compared to the rest of the country, quite clean.

Only when the sun goes down and the cold night air drifts in, does this desert gathering place transform into the most extraordinary of music festivals. This festival is not run according to a strict timetable, and the lineup is a distinctive blend of Touareg and Western music. Malian musicians - greats like Tinariwen and Ali Farka Toure have performed here- alternate with their Western counterparts. Robert Plant has played at the festival, as has Damon Albarn (Gorillaz), along with many others. But the Malian and Touareg musicians are the real draw and the real surprise; some can play traditional music but also blues riffs as well as any American bluesman. While you're warming your hands over the coals, as a seductive Malian sings about life and love, look at the immense desert sky above you and marvel at your good luck.

Voodoo Day

DOLLS STUCK WITH PINS? THAT IMAGE OF VOODOO IS PRIMARILY A PRODUCT OF THE WESTERN IMAGINATION. THE REAL VOODOO, *VODUN*, IS NOT ABOUT JEALOUSY AND PUNISHING YOUR ENEMIES, BUT ABOUT SATISFYING AN INFINITE NUMBER OF SPIRITS. IN BENIN, THE NATIONAL FAITH IS CELEBRATED EVERY YEAR ON VOODOO DAY. THE DAY IS FILLED WITH ANIMAL SACRIFICES, CEREMONIES, AND RITUAL DANCES, WITH RELIGIOUS ECSTASY AS THE ULTIMATE GOAL.

People come to this lively festival in Benin from the surrounding countries in West Africa as well as from countries where the descendants of slaves live, such as Brazil, Haiti and the US, to celebrate their roots and their faith. Benin is the only country where vodun, meaning "spirit" in the local language, is officially recognized and where there is a national holiday to celebrate it.

All over the country, Beninese carry out rituals for the spirits who define man's happiness on earth. The most lavish ceremonies are held in Ouidah, a town on the Atlantic coast from which hundreds of thousands of slaves were shipped to America and the Caribbean. On the beach there is a monument to them, "The gate of no return." During the festival, worshippers circle this gate in a ritual dance, as the roaring crowd cheers along to the drumbeats.

Along the road connecting the town and the beach, the 4 kilometer-long Route des Esclaves, people perform their own little rituals and sacrifice chickens and goats. This dirt road is a sacred place for the Beninese, and you can see talismans and figurines. In addition to these smaller observances, there are more organized ceremonies which vodun high priests and the kings of the various tribes attend. They sit comfortably in the shade of tents, and periodically join in the dancing and the prayers.

Vodun supporters believe that all life is driven by the spiritual forces of natural phenomena like water, fire, earth, and air. They fear that if these forces are not honored with sacrifices, prayers, and rituals, they might disappear or change. Everything has its own mind: a tree, the brook, the road, and it takes some time for the spirits of all these things to absorb what is happening during the ceremonies and to respond with satisfaction or displeasure. This is why you'll see several people collapsing on the ground in religious ecstasy, having been visited by the spirits. People are dancing and dancing and dancing and then – boom! – another one will hit the ground, kicking and turning and wrestling with the spirits. Only to stand up and start dancing again.

03

 BENIN

Ouidah, Benin.

 ORIGIN

Vodun was born from animism and ancestor worship. But when and how the religion specifically became vodun is unclear. It originated in West Africa and spread to Ghana and Nigeria. The slaves took their beliefs to the new world, where vodun developed into the regional forms winti in Suriname and voodoo in Haiti. Vodun in Benin was long forbidden, even though more than sixty percent of the population believes in it. In 1998, the government officially proclaimed January 10th Voodoo Day.

 PARTICIPATE

If you want to know more about vodun, make sure to go to the little Voodoo Museum in Ouidah.

04 Dubai Shopping Festival

WHEN YOU FLY TO THE DUBAI SHOPPING FESTIVAL, MAKE SURE TO TAKE ONLY A CARRY-ON BAG. BECAUSE YOU'LL END UP BUYING EVEN THE NEW SUITCASES THAT YOU'LL NEED TO BRING HOME ALL YOUR NEW PURCHASES. THE DISCOUNTS ARE SO AMAZING THAT YOU MIGHT NOT EVEN PAY ATTENTION TO ALL THE CLOWNS, BALLERINAS AND JUGGLERS THERE TO ENTERTAIN YOU THROUGHOUT THE FORTY MALLS.

Dubai is a mecca of consuming, and every shopaholic should visit it once in his life. Probably it is smartest to make that pilgrimage during Layali Dubai, as the Dubai Shopping Festival (DSF) is called in Arabic. During this time, consumers from all over the world are even more likely to come here to spend their money than during the rest of the year. The red carpets are rolled out and nearly every night dazzling fireworks light up the desert sky, illuminating Dubai's ambitious collection of skyscrapers. Near every mall food court, meeting point, and marble entry hall, there are jugglers, clowns, and acrobats ready to entertain the shoppers. Dance groups, stilt-walkers and musicians provide a well-needed diversion from the frenzied activity taking place inside the brand-name stores. Even the most experienced shopper will need to slow down and catch his breath in Dubai. If you keep a strict schedule and race through the sprawling malls, you still won't manage to hit all the shops, ranging from the super-luxury to spice stands in a souk.

Several lotteries are held during DSF. The cars and cash prizes are often won by one of the many Asian workers who build and mantain the Dubai shopping paradises for very low wages and in bad conditions. Hence DSF's claim that it makes dreams come true, even those of the poor.

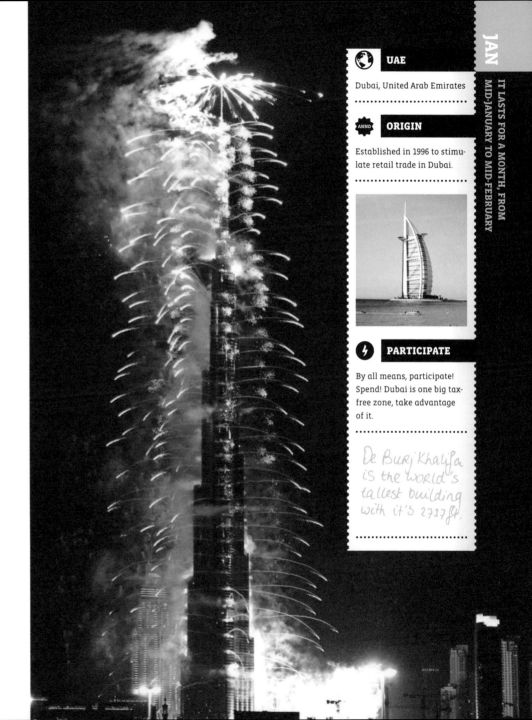

The number of visitors to DSF and amount of money spent are just as staggering as everything else in Dubai. When the festival began in 1996, 1.6 million people spent 430 million euros (€269 per person). In 2009, 3.35 million people came to the festival and spent 1.96 billion euros, €585 per person. And just a few more astounding numbers to chew on: the Mall of the Emirates is 233,000 square meters (including a 14-screen movie theater and a fancy hotel), The Dubai Mall is 440,000 square meters, and Deira City, with only 370 shops in 115,000 square meters, is the baby of the group of malls. Fortunately, all these malls are air-conditioned. Dubai winters can seem chilly compared to the blazing summers but, nevertheless, it's still hot enough to create sweat marks on your new dress. And sweat marks just won't do in Dubai. Naturally, most people just hop into an air-conditioned taxi before taking even one step outside one of the malls.

Over the years, this extravaganza has been expanded to include more activities, such as fashion shows and a jazz festival. And, while you're in Dubai, you can also take a tour to see what this oasis of glass, steel, concrete and marble is actually built on. In the distance, but not so far away, there is only a gorgeous, barren desert and not a mall in sight.

🌐 **UAE**

Dubai, United Arab Emirates

⚙ **ORIGIN**

Established in 1996 to stimulate retail trade in Dubai.

⚡ **PARTICIPATE**

By all means, participate! Spend! Dubai is one big tax-free zone, take advantage of it.

De Burj Khalifa
is the world's
tallest building
with it's 2717 ft.

Harbin Ice Festival

THERE ARE SOME BENEFITS TO TRULY FREEZING WINTERS – TAKE, FOR EXAMPLE, THE ICE AND SNOW SCULPTURES OF THE ICE FESTIVAL IN HARBIN, A CITY IN FRIGID NORTHEASTERN CHINA. SPECTACULAR BUILDINGS MADE OF ICE RISE, LIKE FAIRYTALE CASTLES, ABOVE THE TOWN'S HODGEPODGE OF OLD CHINESE BUILDINGS AND MODERN SKYSCRAPERS.

05

HARBIN

A 820-feet-long and 28-feet-high work of art with an olympic theme made it to the Guinness Book of World Records as the biggest snow sculpture ever. More than six hundred artists helped create it.

In an especially cold winter, temperatures can drop below negative forty degrees Celsius here, so the Songhua River has no difficulties whatsoever in providing the enormous heaps of ice that are needed to sculpt the ice town. With heavy artillery – such as huge drills and saws – the laborers venture onto the frozen river to carve out tons of ice so the ice-artists can begin their work. However, this festival is not only about finely-crafted details, but also about overwhelming size.
You can meander through colossal ice castles and also rocket down ice slides that are so big they would not stand out in the largest of waterparks. You'll also see towering ice pagodas and massive snowmen with faces the size of a window at Macy's. There are ice sculptures in several parks

in Harbin, but the biggest attraction is the park called The Big World of Ice and Snow - a veritable Disneyland of ice. Up to fifteen thousand people have worked day and night in the month before the festival to draw over one hundred thousand cubic feet of water out of the river, to collect snow, and to make the special clear, transparent ice out of demineralized water. The ice-sculptors shape the cold material into architectural wonders: old temples, Russian churches, French cathedrals, new houses, beautiful dolls, exotic animals and summery scenes. And all of this is beautifully illuminated by lights that are strategically placed within the ice to show off the sculptures to their best effect.
If you find yourself getting too carried away by

the ice and the magical lights and starting to daydream, you can always wake yourself up by taking a plunge in the freezing Songhua. Polar bear swimming is what the Chinese call it. The elderly, especially, believe in the healing powers of a quick dip in a pool cut out from the ice. It's good for the blood circulation and the skin, they claim. On some days, there are organized swimming contests, but you can always go and take a dive by yourself.

Chinese New Year

WHEREVER FIRECRACKERS GO OFF IT'S SAFE – SINCE IT'S BELIEVED THAT WHERE A CHINESE FIREWORK EXPLODES, THE EVIL SPIRITS WON'T DARE TO SHOW UP. WHICH MAKES HONG KONG THE PERFECT PLACE TO BE FOR CHINESE NEW YEAR. IN ADDITION, EVERYTHING IS BEAUTIFULLY DECORATED, EVERYONE IS JOYOUS AND, IF YOU BEHAVE CORRECTLY, YOU CAN REST ASSURED THAT THE COMING YEAR WILL TREAT YOU WELL.

Around New Year, the big cities of China are almost impenetrable due to the crowds, so the journey to wherever you are trying to go is quite an adventure. The Chinese have seven days off around New Year, and every day something else is celebrated and another god is worshipped. Everyone wants to go home to see their families and celebrate together, and 'everyone' in China is a massive amount of people. Bus and train stations are insanely packed. Since all the seats have been booked months in advance, those tourists who decide to travel last minute will likely end up sitting on their backpacks in a train station. At this time, the Chinese decorate the streets together, eat together, and they even clean their houses very thoroughly together in order to sweep away any bad fortune to make way for good luck in the coming year. They also go to the temple together and pass each other the traditional little red envelopes *(lai see)* that contain money. Keep in mind that the amount of money must be an even number, also in the dozens; amounts like thirty and fifty are reserved for funeral envelopes.

JAN

AT THE BEGINNING OF THE FIRST CHINESE MONTH, JANUARY OR FEBRUARY.

🌐 CHINA

Hong Kong and the rest of China; wherever there is a big Chinese community.

ANNO ORIGIN

A fight with the mythical beast Nien is believed to have initiated the celebration of Chinese New Year. Nien used to come on the first day of New Year to feast upon livestock and, if he was really hungry, upon the villagers as well. To protect themselves, the villagers put food in front of their doorsteps, hoping that would please Nien. Then a couple of people saw that Nien fled from a little child who was wearing red. From that moment on, they began putting up red lanterns by their houses on New Year's Day and decorating their doors with red paper. The beast Nien never came back again.

⚡ PARTICIPATE

Witness the parade in Hong Kong and you will feel like part of the city. Buy fireworks yourself and hand out little red envelopes with a couple of bucks (even numbers!) to the receptionist of your hotel or hostel (giving envelopes to random strangers is not done). Eat the traditional dishes such as *jiaizo* (dumplings) and *nian gao* (sweet rice pudding), as the Chinese do. Go to one of the temples on New Year's Day to pray with the Chinese. Check **www.gohongkong.about.com** for a schedule of the festivities.

Throughout China the streets are marvelously adorned with fans, lanterns, lights, red paper strips, and beautiful flowers. In Hong Kong, the Chinese go to the flower markets on New Year's Eve to hunt for the most dazzling, colorful bouquets for their family and friends. Around eight p.m., a famous parade begins in Tsim Sha Tsui, the spacious neighborhood close to the water. Floats, lights, drum bands, and impressive classic costumes and dances – like the lion and the dragon dance – are all a part of this incredible spectacle. Hundreds of thousands of people come out to catch a glimpse of the parade and to enjoy the atmosphere. And of course there are phenomenal fireworks. Because without these evil-spirit-chasing explosives, your year will not be blessed with happiness.

07 Timkat

FOLLOWERS OF GOD CAN SOMETIMES
SOUND AS LOUD AS THE MOST FERVENT
SPORTS FANS CELEBRATING A VICTORY.
DURING TIMKAT CELEBRATIONS IN
ETHIOPIA, THOUSANDS OF THE FAITHFUL
WALK FOR HOURS, SINGING AND DANCING,
TOWARDS THE WATER.

During Timkat, the *tabot*, a model of the Ark of the Covenant that is housed
in every church, is carried above surging crowds to a nearby pool of water
or river. The body of water represents the Jordan River, because it's during
Timkat that Orthodox Christian Ethiopians celebrate – and reenact – Jesus'
baptism.

On the eve of Timkat, priests wearing elaborate ceremonial robes carry the
tabot to the water in a colorful procession. All night, the priests watch over
the tabot, which has been placed in a special tent. Flags, lanterns and many
candles provide a little Christmas spirit (Timkat is, after all, the Ethiopian
celebration for Epiphany so Christmas has only just finished) and many of
the faithful camp out nearby. Once the sun has risen, the high priest blesses
the water and the children can then jump in. Adults who prefer to keep their

ETHIOPIA

Gondar, Ethiopia. Also in
Addis Ababa and Lalibela.

ORIGIN

Christianity was already
declared the state religion
of Ethiopia by the year 330.

clothes dry stretch out their arms to be sprinkled with the holy water, since it's believed that if the water touches you, you are free from sin. Those who fully submerge themselves are believed to have renewed their relationship with God.

To catch the sacred drops, everyone pushes and pulls and throws elbows, like women at a designer sample sale. Yet, despite this, Timkat remains a joyful festival. After the splashing and swimming, the parade begins again. The people sing and dance and stomp their feet through the dusty streets, until each tabot is safely returned to its home church.

08

Ati Atihan

 PHILIPPINES

Kalibo, Panay Island, the
Philippines

 ORIGIN

The Spanish Christians tried
to convert the locals to their
God and only agreed to
allow Ati Atihan to continue
if some Christian elements
were incorporated. Calling
it Santo Niño appeared to
be a fine compromise for all
involved.

 PARTICIPATE

Do you like to wear a
disguise? If so, then don't
hold back. Do you want to
run around in a Star Trek
suit? No worries. No one will
look strange at you. Many
youngsters don't wear the
traditional dress anymore
and instead turn Ati Atihan
into their own modern version of Mardi Gras.

SADSAD – DANCING IN THE STREET – IS THE
MOST IMPORTANT WORD TO KNOW DURING
ATI ATIHAN. ADMITTEDLY, SOME RELIGIOUS
SERVICES ALSO TAKE PLACE DURING THIS
FESTIVAL, BUT IT IS REALLY ALL ABOUT THE
STREET PARTIES, THAT GO ON LATE INTO
THE NIGHT.

Necklaces made of bones, sticks with craniums on top, and costumes with skulls are all common accoutrements. Bamboo, feathers, shells - none of it looks very Christian. Nevertheless, during this festival, Santo Niño, the In-fant Jesus, is worshipped. All the masses are dedicated to him, and his image is paraded through the streets. However, indecent behavior is not frowned upon during this celebration. In fact, Ati Atihan is all about stomping your feet, dancing, making music, and overindulging in food and drink.
Ati Atihan means 'like Ati', which is the name for the Philippine island of Panay's native black population. In the thirteenth century, a group of Malay-sians, with a lighter skin tone, ended up on Panay. The Ati, who lived in the mountains, sold a piece of land near the shore to these newcomers. The Ma-laysians were so pleased that a party broke out, during which the newcom-ers painted themselves darker as a tribute to their hosts. Even today, the locals still rub themselves with soot to dance amongst the fire-breathers. After the Spanish settled in the Philippines, the Christian elements of the festival were added.

The entire festival lasts just a week, but it only gets wild the last three days. On Friday morning, there is a serious mass.
Drum groups start their rhythmic hammering, bands start playing and there is *sadsad* until dawn on Saturday morning. Sunday morning there is an open air mass in the Pastrana park. On that same afternoon, a fantastic ceremony takes place, during which multiple tribes compete for various prizes. This ceremony is all about the outfits, the choreography, and the overall performance. If spectators along the side want to join in, that's fine. The more, the merrier, the performers say.

CANADA

Québec, Canada.

TIPS

Caribou (named after a type of reindeer) is the unofficial drink of the festivities. It's an alcoholic mixture that warms the heart. The recipe below will make enough for ten people:

- 9 centiliter Vodka
- 9 centiliter Cognac
- 3.5 deciliter Canadian sherry
- 3.5 deciliter Canadian Port

Throw everything together, mix well, pour into small glasses.

ORIGIN

The first major Winter Carnival was organized in 1894 but, due to the two wars and other economic hardships, it was only organized sporadically over the subsequent 60 years. In 1954, some local businessmen wanted to give Quebec an economic boost and they organized the event again. There was a mascot chosen, Bonhomme – a good marketing tool - and the first version of the re-launched Winter Carnival was held in 1955.

Québec Winter Carnival

09

WITH IGLOOS, LIGHTED ICE PALACES, DANCING SNOWMEN, AND SNOW SLIDES, QUÉBEC IS TRANSFORMED FOR SEVENTEEN DAYS EVERY WINTER INTO A FAIRYTALE LAND. FOR THE CITY'S SHOPKEEPERS, RESTAURANT OWNERS, AND HOTEL WORKERS, WINTER CARNIVAL IS ALSO A CAPITALIST MIRACLE.

French immigrants settled in Québec in the 16th century, which explains the old streets full of fabulous brick buildings and the beautiful castle that looms high on the hill. During the Carnival, the whole town is dedicated to this winter celebration. Everywhere there are lights, Christmas trees, and reindeer junk.

The heart of this festival can be found not on the streets but on (and in) the ice. There are large water slides built of snow and ice. You can build snowmen in a hot tub while the sun sets, climb icebergs, or explore igloos. There's a winter garden where you can watch ice sculptures being built. Should you be in a competitive mood, you can watch or participate in any number of contests: racing with sled dogs, paddling in ice canoes, and, naturally, playing in the hockey rink. This carnival, whose organizers have carefully selected the event's traditions and symbols, has its own parade. You can also take advantage of outdoor concerts and dancing under the cold winter sky. Just make sure to pour some rum in that hot chocolate.

Thaipusam

10

STACKING A FEW STURDY FISH HOOKS ON THEIR CHESTS OR HOISTING HEAVY RACKS ON THEIR NECKS: TAMIL HINDUS HAPPILY ENDURE INCREDIBLE SUFFERING TO ENSURE THAT THE GOD MURUGAN WILL BE MERCIFUL IN THE COMING YEAR.

Murugan, the youngest son of Shiva and the most important god for the Tamils, is pleased when his worshippers undertake arduous tasks for him. The faithful believe that the heavier the burden they haul, the more wealth and health Murugan will bestow upon them. The burden that worshippers each carry is called a *kavadi* and is chosen by the believers. Some types of kavadi can be quite simple, such as a pot of milk. But a number of devotees will opt to carry an elaborate canopy, decorated with flowers and colorful divine images, on their heads to the temple. Those who really desire to win the favor of Murugan will pierce their skin, tongue, or cheeks with skewers, or put a hook in their torso and connect the hooks and piercings to the canopies on their heads. Naturally, these mortifications of the flesh are undertaken without anesthesia.

Thaipusam is celebrated everywhere that Tamils reside. This includes Sri Lanka and India, where the Tamils originally hail from, but also countries to which they emigrated in large numbers, including Mauritius, Singapore, and

🌐 MALAISIA

The Batu caves, just outside Kuala Lumpur, Malaisia. Thaipusam is also observed in other countries with large Tamil communities.

....

🏵 ORIGIN

Thaipusam has been celebrated in Kuala Lumpur since 1982, when the first groups of Tamil came to live in Malaysia. It is said that two Tamils made the heavy climb up to the Batu caves – at that time, there was no staircase- and they left the *vel*, the lance that is symbol for Murugan, in one cave. The cave, roughly the size of a football field, now houses a temple devoted to Murugan.

....

👍 TIPS

Witness this religious phenomenon from up close in the cave or on the stairway leading up to the cave. But keep in mind that the later in the day it gets, the busier it becomes, and in the cave there are lots of people and lots of shoving. Those who get uncomfortable in crowds, should stay close to the exit.

....

Malaysia. In Malaysia, hundreds of thousands of devotees undertake a massive pilgrimage from a temple in the capital city of Kuala Lumpur to the Batu caves, fifteen kilometers away. The night before the procession, an image of Murugan is brought from the city to the cave by a silver carriage; upon seeing the carriage, thousands of onlookers sacrifice coconuts alongside the road. On the day of the pilgrimage itself, the pilgrims, bearing their kavadi, climb the grueling 272 step stairway that leads to the Temple Cave. Everyone is allowed to enter the cave. But don't expect to see ten thousand pierced faces. Only the very dedicated Tamils take that step. To be able to do this, they must abstain from earthly pleasures for 48 days prior to Thaipusam: no meat, no sex, and some even forego sleeping in their beds and sleep on the floor instead. It is believed that only through these deprivations can they enter the necessary trance on the day of the pilgrimage that will enable them to carry their burden. There is a saying that claims, "if you're in trance, your cheeks will not bleed."

Up Helly Aa

JUST ABOUT EVERY MAN FROM THE TINY TOWN OF LERWICK SEEMS TO DRESS UP AS A VIKING ON THIS DAY OF THE YEAR. THESE COSTUMED WARRIORS PARADE THROUGH THE STREETS CARRYING TORCHES THAT THEY WILL THROW INTO A REPLICA VIKING SHIP AT THE END OF THEIR PROCESSION. NATURALLY, OF COURSE, THERE IS ALSO A FAIR AMOUNT OF BEER DRINKING AND DANCING.

Lerwick is in the Shetland Islands, northeast of Scotland, a stone's throw from Norway. Logically, then, the Viking influence is still quite pronounced in this part of the world. Up Helly Aa is the yearly day on which these islanders celebrate their Norwegian heritage. Thousands of men parade through the streets, divided into squads of about twenty five men, and each with its own costume. While old-fashioned Viking regalia predominates, you will see a range of costumes; you might even catch a glimpse of a roguish Mexican hidden among the Norsemen. The most important man of the day is Guizer Jarl, essentially the prom queen, who is flanked by his own squad of *guizers* (men in disguise). To be named Guizer Jarl is the biggest honor that one can achieve here; a strong lobby, the right friends, and years of devotion are all necessary to get elected. You will also need some digits in your bank account, because

11

SCOTLAND

Lerwick, Shetland Islands, Scotland.

 ORIGIN

The festival has existed since 1880, which was a considerable amount of time after the last Viking disappeared. Up Helly Aa seems to have its origins in Yule, the Viking celebration of light that was held after the winter solstice. The act of setting fire to a galley on which they labored for four months likely comes from the ritual of Norwegian tribal chiefs who were cremated on their own ships.

 PARTICIPATE

One of the parties after the torch parade is at the community hall and is open to everyone. You should make a reservation to get a ticket. You can do that starting around Christmas at **www.uphellyaa.org.** For the other parties, the trick is to get in line early and hope that you can get in.

Guizer Jarl and his men are expected to show up in brand-new outfits, their Viking suits kitted out with gleaming new buckles and accessories.

The thousand guizers have a busy schedule. The first procession starts early in the morning, and then the men parade from one official meeting to another. After all these meetings comes the revelation of the year's humorous bill. The bill is a placard on which the government used to post official announcements for the townspeople. These days, the bill is filled with satirical jokes about the locals, and every year the honor of creating the bill goes to a different artist.

The audience, after enduring a bit of shivering alongside the road before the parade, is mesmerized by the torch-lit procession. As evening falls, the spectators ooh and aah as the magnificent Viking galley is devoured by the flames. And then the real party starts. There is eating, drinking, and dancing. Each squad pays a visit to the twelve party halls and the visits don't finish until around eight in the morning. The day after Up Helly Aa is an official holiday in Lerwick so that everyone can recover from the festivities.

Jokkmokk Marknad

THIS ONE IS NOT FOR ANIMAL RIGHTS ACTIVISTS. AT THIS MARKET IN THE FAR, FAR NORTH, EVERYTHING IS ABOUT ANIMAL HIDES. REINDEER SLIPPERS, SHOES, HATS, MITTENS AND LITTLE BOXES MADE OF REINDEER HORNS – YOU WILL SEE IT ALL. YOU MIGHT EVEN FIND THE HIDES OF FOXES, BEARS AND DOGS. HAMBURGERS MADE OF REINDEER MEAT ROUND OUT THE OFFERINGS. ON TOP OF ALL THAT, YOU CAN ALSO HAVE ANIMALS PULL YOU AROUND BY SLED.

12

🌐 SWEDEN

Jokkmokk, Sweden

....

👍 TIPS

A few years ago, the tourist agency of Jokkmokk added a historical market to the regular market. Starting on Sunday evening, the trading rituals of the 17th century are reenacted. At the same time, you can also do some skiing, enjoy old-fashioned beverages and watch movies about life in the old days. Check **www.jokkmokks-marknad.com** to learn more about the special activities.

....

⚡ PARTICIPATE

Try out the reindeer dishes, get a Sami outfit, and let the dogs or reindeer pull you through the beautiful white landscape.

....

⊛ ORIGIN

The permanent market was founded by the Swedish king in the beginning of the 17th century. The location was chosen since it was close to the winter settlements of the wandering Sami; they always visited their friends and relatives at this time of year. The goal of this annual market was to get a better idea of the population in the far north in order to collect more taxes, to administer justice, and to spread the word of God.

....

Jokkmokk is a tiny town in Northern Sweden that is almost permanently covered by a layer of snow. It's essentially a street with some wooden houses, two churches, a restaurant, a hotel, and that's about it. Only during the yearly Jokkmokk Marnad does this quiet village of three thousand become the economic and social heart of the Lappish territories. Tens of thousands of visitors descend on the town each winter to visit the famous market. The indigenous Sami people were already coming to the market hundreds of years ago. It was the highlight of their year. A time in which people would catch up with long distance relatives, do their shopping, and sell their own goods. Even today there are still a lot of Sami wandering about in the market places, looking perhaps for a new knife, a new drinking cup, a nice scarf or maybe a warm hat made of reindeer fur. It's the Sami who sell the goods and who tell the stories, make the music and dance in the evenings in the warmed teepee village.

Night comes early, since February days only last a few hours in Jokkmokk. If you're lucky, you may see some colorful traces of the northern lights in the sky. During the market, the people of Jokkmokk make good use of the few hours of daylight available. There are reindeer races through an obstacle course, children play Sami games, and you can even explore the white lowlands of Jokkmokk in a sled pulled by huskies or reindeer.

In the deep darkness of the evenings, the sparkling fires are especially beautiful. You can huddle by the campfires with a warm drink, tap your feet to the Sami songs, and dance in the warm teepees. And, when all of this comes to an end, you can shuffle back to your nearby hotel or hostel. A walk through the peaceful white landscape, sliding in your new reindeer boots while your breath swirls in little clouds in front of you, is truly unforgettable.

Tapati

EASTER ISLAND IS THE ISLAND WHERE EVERYTHING IS ALMOST EXTINCT, RIGHT? THERE ARE ACTUALLY STILL A FEW THOUSAND RAPA NUI PEOPLE LEFT ON THE ISLAND, AND DURING THE TAPATI FESTIVAL THESE ISLANDERS CELEBRATE THEIR EXISTENCE WITH EXTRA PRIDE AND CONVICTION, WEARING ONLY RATTAN SKIRTS (OR LESS).

Eight banana tree trunks are tied together. At the summit of a long, steep hill, a Rapa Nui man, dressed only in a thong, positions himself on the hand-made sled. He leans back on his elbows, as if sunbathing and checking out girls on the beach. But there's actually nothing relaxing about this event. As soon as he's pushed, he's at the mercy of the sled.

At a Ferrari's speed, the sled barrels down the hill; the trick is to stay on it. If the man reaches the bottom of the hill successfully, he jumps off the sled to do a proud dance. He has proven his manhood.

This two week festival consists of all kinds of competitions celebrating the heritage of Easter Island, also known as Rapa Nui. The events include a triathlon in which one needs to swim in a volcanic lake and sail on rattan rafts, among other things. There is stone-chopping, body painting, drawing competitions, and competitive singing and dancing events with awards for the loudest, best and most skilled. There's also a sprinting competition in which the participants have to carry a bunch of bananas over their shoulders, and a cooking competition, in which participants make a stew in

13

Easter Island, Chile.

INTERESTING

The name Easter Island (Paasch-Eyland) was coined by Jacob Roggeveen, the Dutch explorer who bumped into the volcanic island with his three ships on April 5, 1722, Easter Sunday. Rapa Nui means "big rock" in Polynesian. The island was named that by Tahitian sailors in about 1863.

ORIGIN

The festival has been organized since 1975 to celebrate the Ley Pascua, the law that granted the Easter Islanders the right to vote in the Chilean presidential elections. Another goal of the festivities was to attract tourists. Tapati started small, with poem matches and art exhibitions in the community hall of Hunga Roa. Thanks to the enthusiasm of the Rapa Nui, it grew bigger and bigger. These days, the festival even has its own parade, complete with elaborate floats.

an underground stove. The elements of competition can vary year to year, because the organization wants to keep it interesting and enjoyable for the young people. After all, they are the ones who will be tasked with keeping the tradition alive.

Rapa Nui means big rock and is, easily enough, the name of the island, its inhabitants, as well as its language. For all Rapa Nui, Tapati is the most important festival of the year, and many people even fly back to Easter Island to celebrate it with their families and join in the games. Naturally, in Hunga Roa, the only village in Easter Island, there's a party every night. Throughout the two weeks, there are shows with traditional dances and people chanting, theatrical presentations, and even the crowning of the festival queen. And even though the festivities can have a touristy bent, the Rapa Nui aren't doing this only for your money; they are celebrating their own fortune.

Te Matatini

GRAAAAAWW! THE MURDEROUS LOOKS AND RHYTHMICAL STOMPING OF THE NEW ZEALAND RUGBY TEAM HAVE MADE THE *HAKA* FAMOUS AROUND THE WORLD. WITH THIS MAORI DANCE, THE PLAYERS HAVE ALREADY INTIMIDATED THEIR OPPONENTS EVEN BEFORE THE KICKOFF. BUT THE HAKA IS ONLY ONE OF MANY DANCES OF THE INDIGENOUS MAORI PEOPLE. DURING TE MATATINI, YOU CAN ADMIRE ALL THESE SPECTACULAR DANCES.

During the Kapa Haka competitions, the traditional war dance is not demonstrated for an opponent, but for an audience. The dancers appear to form a ball of controlled aggression on the stage. Legs bent, they reach their arms wide open, revealing bare torsos, some covered in tattoos. Threatening screams and clapping on the arms are all a part of it. Occasionally, the dancers will stick out their tongues in a tormenting way, while their eyes seem to spit fire.

But this competition is about victory, not just entertainment. The best group will advance to the next round. The last, most important round is the one at the Te Matatini festival, an event that celebrates Maori performance arts. Once every two years, the best dance groups assemble at Te Matatini to battle for the title and to amuse ten thousand spectators. While the war dance is perhaps the best known, there are all kinds of dances performed across a number of categories.

But where there is competition, particularly when the judges must name a winner, there are also spirited arguments that can sometimes get quite heated. Not every tribe has the same traditions, but they all must adhere to the same set of rules. This complicates things and can lead to controversy. This was the case a while ago with a dance group that had a female narrator. The jury decided that to have a female narrate was against the rules. The group countered that it was their tribe's tradition to have their story told by a woman, but eventually they had to accept their loss. This incident was the catalyst for a big debate about the role of women in Maori society.

As a visitor to Te Matatani, you can experience the best of Maori culture in one place. You'll find the best community singing of big choirs, for example. Even without knowing a word of Te Reo (the Maori language), the songs will give you goose bumps. You will also see the most beautiful tattoos, ranging from a subtle one on a foot to an extravagant work of art covering an entire face. There is also magnificent attire and choreography to enjoy. And of course there is a marketplace filled with Maori handcrafts to bring home. Or you could always leave with a new tattoo. That might just make you as intimidating as one of the war dancers.

14

🌐 NEW ZEALAND

A different tribe hosts the festival each time, so it is always happening in a different place in New Zealand.

·····························

📖 DICTIONARY

Iwi: tribes
Te matatini: many faces
Kapa: to be lined up
Haka: to dance
Kakahu: attire
Aotearoa: New Zealand

·····························

👍 TIPS

Check **www.tematatini. co.nz** for places, data and tickets. You will also find information about other Kapa Haka festivals that are organized year-round.

·····························

⬡ ORIGIN

Te Matatini is an organization that seeks to preserve the Maori culture and bring it to the world's attention. In the 1960s, the first Maori festivals started popping up, and since 1972 the foundation has organized these events on a grand scale.

·····························

NEW ZEALAND

AUCKLAND

TAURANGA

CHRISTCHURCH

DUNEDIN

15 Argungu Fish Festival

Since 1934

A LIVE NILE PERCH WEIGHING OVER 120 POUNDS CAN'T JUST BE PULLED OUT OF THE RIVER. FOR THIS REASON, MOST OF THE TENS OF THOUSANDS OF FISHERMEN IN THIS FEVERISH, HOUR-LONG CONTEST COMPETE IN PAIRS, VYING FOR A MINIBUS AND OTHER PRIZES.

The main prize, along with the minibus, is a cash prize in the amount of around € 7000, along with new fishing materials. This reward attracts fishermen from all over Nigeria to the Malan Fada River . For a Nigerian whose livelihood is based on fishing, winning this prize is simply life-changing. Perhaps it's logical, then, that things can get nasty during that frenzied hour of competition, with the competitors jostling and sometimes hitting each other as they scour the muddy waters for fish. The winner of the 2008 competition was eventually disqualified and thrown in jail after it was discovered that his winning fish was not caught during the competition. In fact, the fish was already dead and placed strategically in the river to resemble a triumphant catch. Since then, the gills of the fish are now checked to be sure they have been recently killed.

According to tradition, the biggest fish is still reserved for the local ruler, who watches the competition from his shaded throne. When a fisherman comes out of the river with his fish, he is escorted by the elegant and colorfully-dressed guards on horseback to the ruler's throne. This fish hunt is the highlight of the five day festival in Argungu. At this unusual event, you will find rulers and their followers parading around on beautifully dressed horses and camels. Elsewhere, you will see people competing in the sport of dambe, the local form of boxing, to the sound of beating drums. There is also a market that goes on late into the night, and many other forms of entertainment, including a street artist whose empty car runs on nothing more than recitations from the Koran. All of this takes place to the amusement and awe of the hundreds of onlookers.

 NIGERIA

Argungu, Nigeria

....

 PARTICIPATE

Although it is unlikely that you will be forbidden to jump in the river to join in catching the fish, your presence in the water will probably not be appreciated. For fishermen, the contest can be a very serious attempt to make much-needed money.

....

 ORIGIN

Sultan Hasan dan Mu'azu Ahmedu visited the town of Argungu in 1934 and, naturally, a big celebration was made in his honor. The locals immediately organized a major fishing competition, and the largest catch was given to the sultan.

....

FROM WEDNESDAY TO SATURDAY, SOMETIME IN FEBRUARY OR MARCH. PLEASE NOTE, HOWEVER, THAT IT HAS BEEN CANCELLED AT LEAST ONCE DUE TO LOW WATER LEVELS IN THE RIVER.

Rio Carnival

AIAIAI... DURING CARNIVAL, RIO IS THE HOTTEST PLACE IN THE WORLD. FOR FOUR DAYS, SWEAT DRIPS THROUGHOUT THE STREETS OF RIO. DUE TO THE SUN, THE HUSTLE AND BUSTLE OF THE CROWD, THE SAMBA, AND THE PASSION OF THE FESTIVAL.

A million tourists join seven million cariocas during these four days of excitement and never-ending drum beats. Everyone is brought together, dancing exuberantly, while following behind the street bands. There are over 300 of these bands present – from the huge, renowned bands to the unknown street groups.

The bands move through the neighborhoods, from the favelas (Rio's slums) in the hills down to the beach, announcing their presence with loud drumming. Like the Pied Piper, the bands lure the people to the streets, and the mass of partygoers grows. Throughout the city, street parties break out in squares and along street corners, complete with beer and dancing. There are many organized festivals that include bars, stages, and good sound systems. When the sun goes down, the party really gets started, bubbling out of the favelas, across the city, and onto the beach. Each night there are parties in virtually every club, bar, and hotel lobby in town. From the elderly American tourists who've arrived on cruise ships to the drug dealers in the slums, there is a party for everyone.

The music of choice for Carnival in Rio is, naturally, samba. This typical Brazilian mix of swirling beats with African roots is the pulse of Carnival and what brings it its worldwide fame. The highlight of the four days of parties can be found in the Sambodromo. Yes, let that word sink in - Sambodromo. Only in Rio could you find seventy thousand people packed into an incredible samba stadium, singing and dancing. Needless to say, these seats are sold out well in advance.

The Sambodromo is a long, concrete runway strip with stadium seating on

16

BRAZIL

Rio de Janeiro, Brazil

TIPS

Although the parade through the Sambodromo is the highlight for Brazilians during Carnival, you can still have a great experience without expensive tickets. It's free to enjoy on the streets. Check the Carnival website for more information about organized street parties.

PARTICIPATE

For the street parties, you need nothing more than the desire to party. Curvy hips are welcomed, but certainly not required. For those who want to go all out, you can go months in advance to any of the samba schools that also allow tourists, but it is required to rehearse for months before the event. The organization that oversees Carnival in Rio also has a less time-consuming option. At **www.rio-carnival. net**, you can buy a spot in the parade that goes through the Sambodromo. Your ticket: a costume, which you can bet will cost hundreds of Euros. There are only a few samba schools that participate in this deal, but it goes without saying that they will be specific in dictating what costume you wear. You need to do nothing more than just show up a few hours before the parade to quickly learn 3 steps.

both sides for spectators. Samba schools from all over parade down the runway with hundreds of their members, to wild cheers. For months, these schools have been preparing - designing costumes, creating large, extravagant parade floats, and memorizing the samba songs and dances that have been choreographed by the Samba Master – for their moment.

The most beautiful woman stands in front of the float, waving her flags, with dancers and drummers following along. The rest of school follows in their wake, all of them beautifully dressed and swinging to and fro. Each school chooses a theme and tries its best to depict a story that is acted out by the dancers. The school that does the best is announced a few days after the parade and is awarded the Carnival crown. The Saturday after the crowning, Rio has little difficulty in heating up the night again as the best samba schools of the year swing one last time through the Sambodromo.

Mardi Gras

ARRIVE IN A GREEDY MOOD, SINCE MARDI GRAS IS NOT ONLY ABOUT COSTUMES BUT ALSO ABOUT GRABBING BAGS FULL OF NECKLACES, COINS, TOYS, AND OTHER TRINKETS.

The masked and elaborately costumed *krewes* of the floats throw all these items from their floats. And the people in the crowds, prepared with empty bags, elbow each other out and beg for all the kitschy items. The krewes organizing the parades often have decades-old reputations to uphold. Each krewe has its own *doubloon* – an old-fashioned name for currency – that changes each year. One side of the purple aluminum coin bears the krewe's logo while the other side displays an image, a clown's face, for example. There are real Mardi Gras doubloon-diehards out there who collect these items, so be prepared to fight for your fair share.

For the not-as-materially minded, Mardi Gras is also a celebration of music and bizarre costumes. If you find one party boring, then you can just head to a different part of town to find the atmosphere that's right for you. Because

🌍 UNITED STATES

New Orleans, Louisiana, USA.

⚡ PARTICIPATE

Put on your most bizarre outfit and dance with the other revelers at the street parties. Or indulge your acquisitive side and try to fill empty bags with beaded necklaces and other stuff thrown from the floats.

👍 TIPS

If you decide not to dress in costume, at least wear the Mardi Gras colors of purple, green, and gold. During the weekend before Mardi Gras, the krewes hold all kinds of great parades. See **www.mardigrasneworleans.com** for the schedule and routes.

⊛ ORIGIN

Mardi Gras is French for Fat Tuesday, the Tuesday prior to the beginning of Lent. The party in New Orleans has a long history. Behind masks, blacks could not be as easily identified and could behave more freely. This grand New Orleans celebration began in 1871. In 1872, the Mardi Gras colors were introduced: purple (justice), green (faith), and gold (power); three years after that, the state of Louisiana declared Mardi Gras a holiday.

Mardi Gras can be as touristy, childish, extravagant, obscure, or sleazy as you want. Besides the krewes who are out on the day of Mardi Gras itself, a few krewes are already out driving through the streets the weekend before Fat Tuesday. And then there are the Mardi Gras Indians who are, quite confusingly, African-American. They wear fantastic costumes and feathers and parade through their neighborhoods.

If you are really seeking the soul of New Orleans, go to the French Quarter in the evening. During the day, people dress up in all kinds of weird costumes, hang out there and dance a bit, but as the day progresses, things get wilder. In exchange for a cheap beaded necklace, girls will famously bare their breasts – a sight that's often captured on camera. Indeed, at Mardi Gras, the higher the blood alcohol content, the more flashes you will see.

Carnaval de Oruro

WHEN YOU WORK IN A MINE, DEEP UNDERGROUND, YOU WILL NEED A SAINT. IN BOLIVIA THIS SAINT IS FETED WITH AN ANNUAL CARNIVAL THAT LASTS THREE DAYS.

Life can be bleak and challenging in Bolivia, but the Oruro Carnival – the biggest annual cultural event in Bolivia – is a time of pure joy. The people dance, sing, then dance some more. Tens of thousands of musicians and dancers take part in a procession that lasts an astonishing twenty hours. It's a never-ending parade of different costumes, one more ornate than the next: short skirts and gold boots, big Indian headdresses, huge animal heads, glittered dresses, traditional pieces, and, lastly, the devil suits. La Diablada, the Dance of the Devils, is one of the major components of this carnival. Lucifer and Satan lead the way, followed by the devil women. The women are then followed by the seven deadly sins, and behind them come the dancing children. Throughout the dance, angels and demons constantly circle and confront each other, and the forces of good ultimately defeat the Devil.

FEB

SATURDAY AND SUNDAY BEFORE ASH WEDNESDAY (IN FEBRUARY OR MARCH).

 BOLIVIA

Oruro, Bolivia.

⚡ **PARTICIPATE**

Watch, drink, and enjoy. On the Tuesday before Ash Wednesday, families burn small packages to encourage happiness and prosperity. These are offerings to Mother Nature in gratitude for all she's given. The packages often consist of llama dung, incense, sweets, peas, rice, and fake gold and silver. Locals will also pour some alcohol on the ground.

👍 **TIPS**

Oruro is located at roughly 3710 meters above sea level, which is very high. Take a few days to acclimate, especially if you're planning on drinking lots of alcohol during the fiesta.

ANNO **ORIGIN**

According to the legend, a thief called Chiru-Chiru was fatally wounded and the Virgen de la Candelaria stayed with him in a mineshaft until he died. When the miners came upon the lifeless body of Chiru-Chiru, an image of the Virgin suddenly appeared on the wall. From then on Virgin of Candelaria was also called the Virgen del Socavon, Our Lady of the Mineshaft, and she is worshipped as the patron saint of all miners.

Spaniards banned the rituals of local people, the Uru, in the 17th century. One of these rituals was a dance to honor the god of lakes, rivers, and mines. The Spanish attached a saint to this religious ceremony, hence the celebration for Our Lady of the Mine Shaft. But the Spanish weren't able to fully erase all traces of the original ritual - miners in the parade still offer their best minerals to El Tío, the evil ruler of the subterranean world according to the Uru. At the end of the festival, there is a mass to honor Our Lady of the Mine Shaft, then the splendid costumes and props are put away and the residents of Oruro return to their everyday existence.

Pasola

THE PRESENCE OF THE SEA WORMS INDICATES TO THE PRIESTS THAT IT'S TIME FOR THE SPEAR FIGHT. NO SEA WORMS, NO FIGHT. IF THERE ARE SEA WORMS, THE FIGHT BEGINS AND HUNDREDS OF SPEARS FLY THROUGH THE AIR. SOMETIMES THESE WEAPONS HIT THEIR TARGETS; ANY BLOOD THAT FLOWS ONTO THE GROUND IS BELIEVED TO FERTILIZE THE EARTH. THE SPILLED BLOOD PREDICTS THAT THE COMING YEAR IS GOING TO BE A GOOD ONE. – HURRAY!

The most violent element has been removed from Pasola - the wooden spears cannot have sharpened tips anymore. Yet this battle on horseback between two groups of men is still quite rough. On top of that, fighting is in the blood of the islanders of Sumba, in Indonesia. As Sumba is quite isolated from other islands, vicious conflicts between rival clans were still known to break out quite often until only recently.

Christians only set foot on the island's shores quite late, which explains the continued strength of animistic beliefs among the islanders. Pasola starts

19

FEB

FEBRUARY/MARCH, EIGHT OR NINE DAYS AFTER THE
FIRST FULL MOON OF THE LUNAR CALENDAR -
DEPENDING ON THE SEA WORMS AND THE PRIESTS.

🌐 **INDONESIA**

In different locations on Sumba, Indonesia, including Wanukaka, Lanboya, Gaura and Kodi.

....

⚡ **PARTICIPATE**

Dodge spears and eat fried sea worms

....

Marapu is the local religion on Soemba. The marapu priests decide when Pasola starts.

....

....

out with the nyale, the sea worm. Each year, about eight days after the full moon in spring, the nyale come to the shores of Sumba to mate. The beautiful coastline is then covered by squirming green and grey worms. In the early morning, the local priests from the island villages venture out to the coast to gauge the state of the nyale. Once the coast is full of the creatures, the priests wade into the ocean up to their waists and bring back baskets filled with worms. With their catch they predict the future. Will the rice crop be plentiful? Will the weather be favorable? Will there be war? Disease? When the priests are done predicting, the rest of the village can begin the fight. The nyale in the baskets will be fried and nibbled on later. A nice little snack to enjoy while watching the brutal spear contest.

In the afternoon, the men that have been selected advance to the battleground on their finely- dressed horses. In their hands they hold their ammunition – up to a dozen spears. Both teams line up, at opposite sides of the field, and this lends the first attack a rather orderly aspect. But after that organized start, it becomes completely chaotic; it appears to be every man for himself. The horses make sudden jerks and storm without fear towards their opponents. Spears stream through the air, looking for some human flesh to pierce. Spectators scream when somebody gets jolted off his horse. Although the battle is not as bloody now as in the old days, the people of Sumba still say it's a good sign when some blood is shed. A dead man is not necessarily a bad thing, either. Anyone fancy a fried worm?

Carnevale di Venezia

20

DRESSING UP LIKE MICKEY MOUSE, JAMES BOND OR LADY GAGA IS NOT WHAT ONE DOES IN VENICE. THIS CARNIVAL IS REFINED AND TRADITIONAL. GUESTS – EVER-SO-GLAMOROUS IN WHITE MASKS, GARMENTS COVERED WITH GEMSTONES, AND GLOVES – ENGAGE IN FORMAL DANCING AT ELEGANT BALLS.

A mask has a mysterious air, even when you've seen twenty similar masks in a row. Anonymity has always been a main aspect of carnival here. It allows people from every class to move freely, despite their background, sex, or position. For a while, it was even obligatory for civilians to wear masks when voting so that everyone could vote without fear of repercussions. Rulers with dictatorial tendencies cannot abide anonymity, however, so when Napoleon rose to power, Venice's carnival was seriously restricted. Mussolini always wanted to keep an eye on everyone and completely forbade the festivities during the 1930s.

 PARTICIPATE

Be the belle of the ball and rent or buy a gorgeous outfit. It might be cheaper to do that at home than in Venice, where the prices skyrocket during carnival – although it has to be said that the outfits bought or rented in Venice are truly magnificent. There are still all kinds of mask-makers with their own ateliers and shops in the center of the city. A good one is **www.cartaalta.com**. You can also order a mask from them in advance and have them send it to you.

 TIPS

⚡ Tickets for the balls can be expensive and scarce. If you want to go to one of the parties, be sure to start ticket hunting about six months in advance. One of the most popular parties is Ballo del Doge: **www.ballodeldoge.com**. The Gran Ballo della Cavalchina is held in a theater: **www.teatrolafenice.it**.

⚡ It goes without saying that you won't get into these without proper attire.

⚡ Check **www.carnevale. venezia.it** for the schedule of events, as well as the places and times of the fireworks and other shows.

 ITALY

Venice, Italy.

ANNO **ORIGIN**

The word *carnival* likely originates from the Latin carne vale (the farewell of meat), a reference to the Catholic fasting period – in which no meat is eaten – of Lent. In Venice, the carnival season already gets underway on December 26th and lasts until Ash Wednesday. For years, the citizens were allowed to wear a mask during that entire period. Carnival here really reached its height in the 18th century, when hedonism reigned supreme and the parties were extravagant. The costumes worn today still refer back to those glory days.

Since **1268**

In 1979, the carnival was revived. Ever since, the center of Venice is filled with the most luxurious, theatrical, costumes and masks during the two weeks preceding Ash Wednesday. Piazza San Marco is the center with dozens of costumed performers allowing tourists to take pictures of them as living statues. Tourists, with their simple masks, jeans, and fanny packs, make up a sizeable portion of the revelers, although there are thousands of Venetians celebrating, also. Gondolas float through canals filled with beautiful creations, and there is live music on the streets as well as open air shows. Anyone who walks around without a mask will be asked every hundred meters if he wants to have some makeup applied, and merchants will be ready with their little brushes. When evening falls, it's time for the grand galas. You will only be let in if you have a ticket and if you're decked out in proper Venetian carnival attire. If you don't want to be the outcast, you should also practice the quadrilles and other dances in advance with the help of YouTube.

La Battaglia delle Arance

THE RESULT OF OF AN UNPEELED, SLIGHTLY DRIED ORANGE HITTING YOUR CHEEK AT 40 KILOMETERS AN HOUR? A BRUISE. BUT THOSE WHO LEAVE LA BATTAGLIA DELLE ARANCE WITHOUT SWOLLEN FACES HAVE NOT REALLY EXPERIENCED IT.

Thousands of Italians and tourists gather each year in Ivrea, Italy to fight or to watch this three day orange "war". Starting early in the afternoon, the combatants grab thousands of oranges out of crates and pummel their enemies. The battle, throughout the city's old squares and streets, lasts until the sun goes down and the streets are filled with a sour, slippery orange muck. The battle is between nine teams, some representing the people fighting against tyranny and others portraying the army of the feudal lords. The "noble" teams fight from carts and are allowed to wear masks, while the commoners must throw their oranges from the ground. Colorful costumes evoking the Middle Ages abound. Shopkeepers and residents of the old city board up their windows or protect their buildings with nets to catch flying oranges. Anyone seeking immunity wears the soft red elf hat *(berrettofrigio)* that is for sale everywhere in town during the festival. But if you regret your cowardice and decide to join the fighting, simply remove the hat and, in no time, you'll be part of the action.

Officially, people who are not part of the teams are allowed to join the fight after it's begun. If you really want to spend three days soaking in OJ, then sign up with one of the *aranceri apiedi*, the teams on foot. Everyone is accepted, but you'll have to pay membership fee; the amount varies per team. The money for the fee goes to the clothes, oranges, and cleaning of the squares.

21

🌐 ITALY

Ivrea, an ancient village in northwestern Italy.

👍 TIPS

- ⚡ Wear sturdy shoes, since the ground can get very slippery.
- ⚡ Do you wear glasses? You may need to wear goggles to protect your sight.
- ⚡ Bring some clean, dry clothes.

⚙ ORIGIN

The *Carnevale di Ivrea* includes many days of masquerades, parades, and food and drink festivals. The orange battle, arguably the highlight of the carnival, symbolizes the people's rebellion against the oppressive nobility. That revolt was put in motion by Mugnaia La Violetta, a miller's daughter who, according to the legend, rebelled against the local baron's self-proclaimed right to *prima nocta,* the noble's right to have sexual relations with any newly married woman on the night of her wedding. Violetta not only did not spread her legs for the baron, she cut his head off. And that's how the revolt started.

⚡ PARTICIPATE

- ⚡ Want to throw oranges for three days? Sign up for one of the teams at **www.carnevalediivrea.it**. Expect to pay around 100 euros as a membership fee.
- ⚡ Observing the action is free and there are special stands and spots behind the nets. Or you can risk it and watch from the battlefield itself. Just hope that you will actually be protected by the immunity allowed by your red hat.

☠ 🍺

Hadaka Matsuri

YOU'VE BEEN ALMOST NAKED FOR HOURS IN THE FREEZING COLD AND PRESSED BETWEEN THOUSANDS OF MEN. BUT, A BIT OF OF SAKE MAKES IT ALL MUCH MORE BEARABLE. AND IF YOU'RE LUCKY, YOU MIGHT CATCH ONE OF THE SACRED STICKS THAT PROMISE A YEAR OF GOOD LUCK.

Have you ever seen steam coming off your own body? No? Then this is your chance. Spend a few hours running in only a fundoshi, or Japanese loincloth, through the streets as the mercury hovers right around zero, and you'll become a virtual fog cloud. On your way through the streets, you'll be warmed by the sake and your internal engine, but kindly cooled down by spectators splashing water on you. It's supposed to make you clean and pure, as all the bad in you is washed away. This ritual is only reserved for men. Maybe that is a logical, or maybe it's because the hadaka matsuri (naked festival) could otherwise end in a bloody scene.

At the end of the event, precisely at midnight, the sacred sticks that have

 JAPAN

Saidai-ji-temple, Okayama, Japan

....

 ORIGIN

Hadaka Matsuri is a part of Shinto, the original religion of Japan, in which many different natural spirits are worshipped. Around five hundred years ago, Shinto priests received papers upon the successful completion of their training, and they threw these paper talismans into the crowd of worshippers. Those people who received these papers were believed to have more good fortune in the following years, so more and more people wanted to receive these paper talismans of good luck. Since paper tears easily, sticks where used instead.

....

 PARTICIPATE

Any man can participate. A ticket is not required, but fundoshi and tabi are. There are tents to change in, and volunteers ready to tightly tie the fundoshi on you through your butt crack. Be sure to put on your slippers first as bending with the fundoshi might be challenging. Within the temple grounds, it does get quite rough. For those who don't want to get bruised and the breath knocked out of you, try to stay towards the outer circle of the mass of people.

....

 DICTIONARY

 Shingi: The Holy Stick
 Washoi: A yell meaning 'hooray' or 'fantastic'.

....

been put into position during the temple mass are thrown into the crowd of naked men. If you're lucky enough to get hold of a stick, you must then throw the stick into a special bowl of rice. Only then can your year of happiness and good luck begin. However, you'll have little time to carefully aim the stick into the bowl, as thousands of men will be struggling to take the stick from you.

The density of bodies packed into such a small area is so incredible that a Western European crowd-control agent would be covered in red stains. The huddled mass begins on the streets around the temple, stretches up the temple stairs, and becomes even more densely packed the closer you get to the temple's epicenter. This herd of naked bodies moves as one, swaying like seaweed. If someone falls, he runs the risk of being trampled. Some of the men even start fights. In order to exclude members of the Yakuza (Japanese mafia), men with tattoos are not allowed to participate in hadaka matsuri. You are only allowed to have a small tribal tattoo on your ankle. Your feet are where the tabi – Japanese slippers that separate the big toe from the others – are worn. Women can participate in their own hadaka matsuri, although there is little nudity in those festivals. Instead, the ladies dress in neat clothing and are splashed with cold water.

22

Holi

SO YOU STILL HAVE SOME SKIN SHOWING? NOT FOR LONG. SOON YOU'LL BE COVERED IN POWDERS OF ALL COLORS. CELEBRATING HOLI IN INDIA MEANS AN ENTIRE DAY OF STREET PARTYING COMBINED WITH POWDER AND WATER THROWING.

You'll be sprinkled from the roofs and shot at with water guns. You'll return to your hotel not just multi-colored but also with a hundred new friends since this day is all about laughter and smiling. Water balloons, powder from plastic or paper bags, huge buckets of colored water where each person can refill his buckets and other artillery... Holi is pure, colorful mayhem.

Years ago, the powders and dyes were made from tree and flower petals, but today they contain a considerable amount of chemicals and toxins – the authorities will even warn you about it. Hopefully, a bit of lead powder on your delicate skin will not be too harmful since it's only for one day. Just make sure to apply a mud mask when you get home.

Holi has been celebrated for centuries, and the festival is especially popular in northern India. On the evening preceding the paint festival, big fires are lit to ward off evil. In the weeks before Holi, families build fires together – they do this by throwing something flammable on their pile every day. There are fires in gardens, in the streets, and in town squares. Naturally, eating, drinking, and partying are also integral to this festival. Because when the fire destroys the wood, all evil and worry goes up in smoke. And that's cause for celebration.

In Jaipur, Holi is observed with particular extravagance, in the form of an elephant show. The elephants are dressed up in beautiful pieces of cloth with golden thread and other decorations, their heads used as canvases for bright flower patterns and geometrical figures. In the local stadium, there are even little dance shows – that is, if the chaos allows it. And yes, it is the elephants that dance. The animals also participate in speed contests and do acrobatic tricks. A chaotic elephant polo match is played and the elephants pose for pictures. And don't forget that at the same time there's a war of powder and water going on throughout the entire stadium. *Holi hai!*

23

FEB

ON THE DAY OF THE FULL MOON IN THE HINDU MONTH PURNIMA, USUALLY AT THE END OF FEBRUARY/BEGINNING OF MARCH.

👍 TIPS

The elephant show is free, but crowded and chaotic. Push your way in shamelessly, as the Indians do.

🌐 INDIA

Jaipur, India.

⚡ PARTICIPATE

Buy your own ammunition of colored powder at one of the markets in the days before Holi. Wearing only old rags or clothes you don't care about, venture out onto the streets. Women, keep in mind that, even completely covered in paint, this is still India, so you can likely count on a grab or squeeze that is a bit too intimate along with that color throwing.

🔖 ORIGIN

Like so many Indian festivals, Holi is based on a combination of different legends and spiritual traditions. These days, it is a Hindu festival that is celebrated by Indians of all religions. The campfire symbolizes the struggles of Prahlad, who survived a fire thanks to his strong faith in the god Vishnu. It was also Vishnu who invented the throwing of the colors. He was reincarnated as the jolly brat Krishna who chased giggling girls through the village with paint bombs.

JAIPUR

Jaipur is also known as the pink city. For Indians, pink symbolizes hospitality. When the prince of Wales visited the city in 1876, maharajah Ram Singh had the whole city painted pink. More than a century later, the color still dominates the town.

RUSSIA

Moscow, Russia (and the rest of Russia).

PARTICIPATE

Join the outdoor games, stuff yourself with delicious blinis, and, if you're game, perhaps someone will even be willing to fight with you.

TIPS

Although it is technically a spring celebration, it can still be ice cold during Maslenitsa in Moscow. Make sure to pack your thermal underwear.

DICTIONARY

Maslenitsa is also called the Pancake Week, or Butter Week. The word Maslenitsa derives from the Russian word for butter, *maslo*.

Maslenitsa

WOMEN MAKE BLINIS (RUSSIAN PANCAKES) AND MEN FIGHT EACH OTHER.
SUCH A SPLENDID FESTIVAL, MASLENITSA. A WEEK OF SLEDDING THROUGH
TEMPERATURES WELL BELOW FREEZING, AND, AT THE END OF IT ALL,
THE BURNING OF A STRAW DOLL TO BID GOODBYE TO WINTER!

стенка на стенку is the name of the fighting style in Russian. In English it translates as wall-to-wall. Men gather by street, district, school, or employer and line up opposite each other. Attacking and pounding at will then follows. Complete with bruises, bleeding noses, lost teeth, and bruised ribs, they all then head out to drink vodka. The authorities weren't – and still aren't – very fond of wall-to-wall, and sometimes it was even forbidden. It was replaced by snowball fights, or the men were asked to wear boxing gloves during the fight and to try to restrain themselves a bit. But, regardless of the exact details, Maslenitsa has been at the mercy of many different regimes. It started as a pagan festival to welcome spring. The blinis symbolized the sun: round, yellow, and warm. The straw doll, Lady Maslenitsa, was burned at the end of the festivities, and winter was believed (or hoped) to vanish with her smoke. Her ashes were then buried in the snow to make the earth fertile for the next season.

When the Christians came along, they altered the pagan festival and it became the pre-Lenten celebration of Mardi Gras. All of a sudden, the blinis became dishes made to get rid of the eggs and dairy products rather than the focus of the celebration. Later, the communists showed up and wanted nothing to do with the church, so Maslenitsa wasn't celebrated openly for decades. During the communist years, people celebrated privately by making blinis at home. Only in 2002 was the festival publicly organized again, with great pride.

In some regions, every day of the Maslenitsa week has its own theme: visiting friends, fighting, eating... But, for all regions, the final day is a day of forgiveness. Each person asks his or her friends and family for forgiveness, and is met with the answer, "God will forgive you."

Even now, Maslenitsa remains an outdoor event, even though the temperatures are often far below the freezing point. There are games in the snow and blini feasts in city plazas. In Moscow, near the Red Square, there is even a Maslenitsa village built, complete with little booths, lights, and food stands. Fireworks are lit and Russian music is played. However, if you want to put up a fight, this might not be the right spot for it.

Golden Shears

THINK SHEARING SHEEP IS BORING? KIWIS KNOW HOW TO TURN A SHEARING COMPETITION INTO A THRILLING EVENT. WHILE THE AUDIENCE HOWLS, THE SHEARERS SKILLFULLY SCRAPE THE WINTER COAT OFF THE SHEEP IN JUST A COUPLE OF MINUTES. THE FIRST TO SHEAR FIVE SHEEP CONTINUES ON TO THE NEXT ROUND.

The men are sweating. Backs arched, they bend over the sheep, fear in its eyes, as it is pushed back and forth. The sheep start out on their backs, since the shearers begin with the bellies. The strokes the shearers use to go down the body are as long as possible, line after line. The goal is to cut the wool – the fleece - into long strips. Next to every contestant is a jury member who ensures that the competitor doesn't somehow trick the rest of the participants.

The commentator's voice roars over the buzzing of the trimmers – it's no easy feat to be heard above that din. As quickly as possible, the speaker struggles to comment on each of the seven or eight men on the stage and to also encourage the crowd to cheer for the participants. There are different categories - juniors, amateurs and pros. All of the categories have qualifying rounds and finals, each with its own rules. Most of the qualifying contests consist of shaving five sheep,

with only the fastest shearer making it to the next round. Even more has to be accomplished in the finals, when fifteen sheep need to be sheared. The sheep have been carefully chosen, since they cannot be too different from each other in size and wool. They stand ready in little alleyways behind the stage, the one that is on deck waiting in a little paddock directly behind the shearer. When the shearer is ready for the sheep, he pulls open the little door and pulls the sheep out. As soon as

25

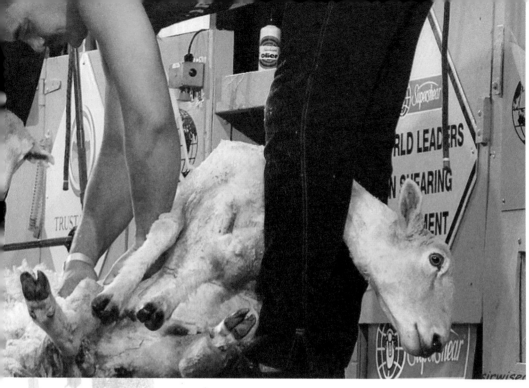

🌐 NEW ZEALAND

Masterton, New Zealand.

👍 TIPS

A ticket for the qualifying rounds costs NZ $ 10; one for the main event is NZ $ 30. Check goldenshears. co.nz for prices, times and data. And if you happen to pass by one of the smaller shearing contests, take the opportunity to watch New Zealanders go into a frenzy over sheep wool.

⊛ ORIGIN

The first big sheep shearing competition was organized in 1958 by members of the Young Farmers' Club. It was a success from the beginning: shearers from all over New Zealand participated. In 1961, the government expected such a huge number of fans that the army was engaged to keep the crowd under control at the stadium. In the years since, the event has expanded to include more days and more categories, as well as other, smaller shearing events.

the wool is off, he pushes the sheep, now bare in its summer outfit, through another door.

After all, as the cliché goes, there are more sheep than people in New Zealand. This is actually true, and perhaps it explains the residents' fondness for the animals. The Kiwis treasure their sheep shearing tradition, so, naturally, the most important shearing contest is broadcast on TV. On top of that, the winners can go on to the world championship, in which more than twenty countries fight for the title.

But this event is not only about the shearers but also about the wool industry. There is also a competition for *wool handlers*, the people who collect and sort the shaved wool, and one for *wool pressers*, those who package the wool. And don't think that any of this is a piece of cake - anything is difficult when you have to do it at lightning speed. Even packing wool can be electrifying to watch when two teams are fighting it out for one trophy.

Chahar Shanbeh Soori

THE HIGHER THE FIRE, THE MORE GUTS IT TAKES TO JUMP OVER IT. DURING CHAHAR SHANBEH SOORI, YOU WILL HAVE MANY OPPORTUNITIES TO DO JUST THAT. EVERYWHERE IN IRAN DURING THIS FESTIVAL, BONFIRES FILL THE STREETS. HE WHO DARES TO TAKE A LEAP IS LOOKING AT A PROSPEROUS YEAR TO COME.

In contemporary Iran, where Islam has been forced upon the people, Chahar Shanbeh Soori is a party that everybody can join, regardless of his or her faith. The celebration is a thousand years old, and many of the same rituals have been practiced since 1700 B.C. The fire symbolizes light and goodness, as well as spring and the longer days that are to come after a harsh winter. The jumping over the fire is a purification ritual. While the Iranians jump they sing: 'sorkhieh tu az man, zardieh man az tu', which translates to "your bright red color is mine, your sickly yellow paleness is yours". This is their way of asking the fire to take away their weakness and to give them strength and energy. Most Iranians likely don't give the ritual's origin a moment's thought when they take the big jump over the fire in their flip-flops; the fire night is mostly a fun neighborhood event.

MAR

THE TUESDAY EVENING BEFORE NOROEZ, PERSIAN NEW YEAR, NORMALLY AROUND MARCH 21ST.

🌐 **IRAN**

Everywhere in Iran

⚙ **ORIGIN**

The festival, or at least a part of it, is almost four thousand years old. Some of the rituals originated during the time in which the Persians followed Zoroastrianism, in which there is a god of good and a god of evil. The Persians believed that the ghosts of their ancestors would visit right before the start of the new year. To protect these ghosts against the god of evil, people lit fires.

TEHRAN

The islamic goverment doesn't really like the secular chahar Shanbeh Soori. The police broke up a couple of street parties in 2010 - some with violence - likely because they were afraid of riots.

IRAN

Schools light little charcoal fires for the toddlers, ladies lift their skirts to attempt a maximum leg spread and to ensure that their dresses do not catch fire. Some families light a campfire in their own gardens, but most of the bonfires occur in the streets. Some make it a social night in which entire streets, neighborhoods and villages catch up and spend time together. Eavesdropping on neighbors' conversations is a part of it. This is called *Fal gush*, listening to your future. If you overhear a positive conversation, your wishes will come true and you will have a good year. But bad luck may be in the cards if you hear someone speaking negatively about you.

Chahar Shanbeh Soori (*soori* means fiery, red) actually falls on a Wednesday before the Persian new year. However, since an Islamic superstition holds that Wednesdays are unlucky days, Chahar Shanbeh Soori is celebrated the night before, on Tuesday night. On that night, Iranians hand out food to neighbors and strangers alike – primarily noodle soup, nut mixes, and dried fruit. Generosity is another way to start the new year on a good note. So make sure to bring something with you that you don't mind giving away.

26

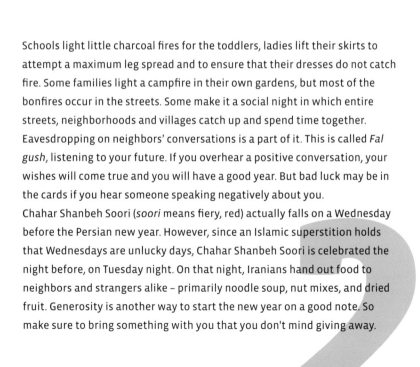

27 Las Fallas

DISNEYLAND MEETS SALVADOR DALÍ AT THIS GIANT SPANISH STREET PARTY. LAS FALLAS IN VALENCIA IS FIVE DAYS FILLED WITH KITSCH, HUMOR, ALCOHOL, AND TONS OF FIREWORKS.

The main focus of the festival is the creation and burning of the *fallas,* towering constructions composed of wood, cardboard, paper-mâché, wax, and plaster. Residents of all 350 districts of Valencia work for up to a year on their own fallas. Well, they raise money with which they pay professionals to build them. There are also fallas made by children. Altogether, the festival features about eight hundred of these sculptures, each with its own story or theme. Only one falla, chosen by the people, will be saved from the ultimate fire and displayed in the Fallero Museum.

Each falla consists of several *ninots* – dolls or figures – and many are satirical in nature. Poking fun at corrupt politicians is always popular. How the fallas came to be the pastel-colored, Disney-style creations they are today is unclear. But it can be said that their kitschy looks make it easier to endure the eventual stabbing of the fallas with sticks of fire, the highlight of the festival. The day of the burning of the constructions is called *La Crema,* and it features (like almost everything else during these five days) a massive

🌐 **SPAIN**	🏵 **ORIGIN**
Valencia, Spain.	Centuries ago, when winter was ending and the days were getting longer, local carpenters burned the wooden structures on which the winter street lamps stood and this became a yearly ritual. The Catholic Church combined the ritual with the day of Saint Joseph, the patron saint of carpenters. Every year the festival became more elaborate, and over the centuries it has grown into the gigantic, fire-filled extravaganza that it is today.

explosion of fireworks and a great deal of shouting. For the five days leading up to La Crema, Valencia is one loud street party. People try to visit as many neighborhoods as they can, to see as many fallas as possible. Each neighborhood holds its own party complete with homemade paella, women in traditional costumes, and a brass band. Every day at exactly 2 p.m., *la mascletà* (an explosion of firecrackers) sounds, and every day there is another parade through the city of people in bright and fanciful costumes. Every night, people dance late into the night on the main square and along the riverbank. And they get up and do it all again the next day. And the day after that. Until there is nothing left of Las Fallas but ash heaps.

28 St. Patrick's Day

AT ONE POINT IT SEEMED LIKE THE WANNABE-IRISH OVERSEAS WERE STEALING ALL THE ST. PATRICK'S DAY GLORY, BUT THEN DUBLIN TOOK MATTERS INTO ITS OWN HANDS. TODAY, IRELAND'S CAPITAL HOSTS A GRAND CELEBRATION COMPLETE WITH A PARADE AND HUNDREDS OF THOUSANDS OF GREEN-CLAD LOCALS AND TOURISTS.

The whole celebration lasts five days, culminating in the major party on March 17. On that day, a parade winds through the center of Dublin, its destination St. Patrick's Church. This is definitely no run-of-the-mill parade, as it features stilt walkers, clowns, floats, marching bands, jugglers, jokers, bagpipe players, and more. Thousands of people line up hours before the noon start time to secure good spots.

The green color for which the day – and Ireland – is famous, comes from the symbol of St. Patrick, the shamrock. According to the legend, St. Patrick used the shamrock to illustrate the doctrine of the Holy Trinity. Needless to say, you'll find more green hats, green "Kiss Me I'm Irish!" t-shirts, green face paint, inflatable green shamrocks and other knickknacks for sale than you could ever wish for. So, if you arrive at the event in an outfit that is not green, rest assured that you can buy yourself an entirely new, green ensemble. In Temple Bar, the entertainment district, the day is one big street party. Even if it rains, everyone simply opens up their green umbrellas and keeps partying. There is green beer to drink and cabbage to eat, should you so choose. And then there is more beer. You can also enjoy live music everywhere on the streets.

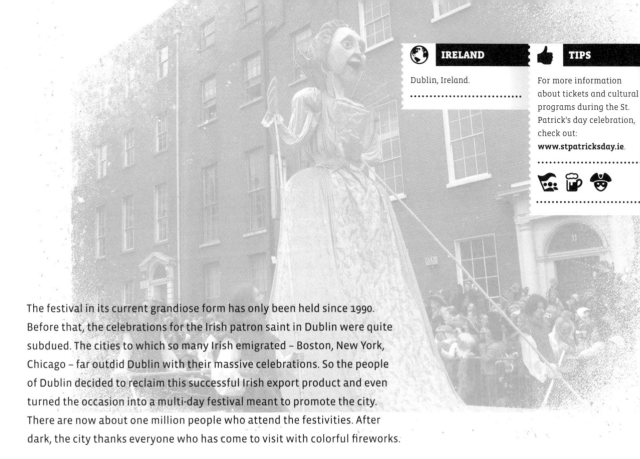

IRELAND

Dublin, Ireland.

TIPS

For more information about tickets and cultural programs during the St. Patrick's day celebration, check out: **www.stpatricksday.ie**.

ORIGIN

Patrick is believed to have been born in the fourth century, the child of wealthy British parents. At sixteen he was kidnapped by Irish thugs and taken to Ireland. God told Patrick in a dream how he could escape: go to the coast and there will be a ship waiting for you. Later in life he returned to teach people in Ireland Catholic beliefs and values.

The festival in its current grandiose form has only been held since 1990. Before that, the celebrations for the Irish patron saint in Dublin were quite subdued. The cities to which so many Irish emigrated – Boston, New York, Chicago – far outdid Dublin with their massive celebrations. So the people of Dublin decided to reclaim this successful Irish export product and even turned the occasion into a multi-day festival meant to promote the city. There are now about one million people who attend the festivities. After dark, the city thanks everyone who has come to visit with colorful fireworks.

Humorina

SECRETLY TYING SOMEONE'S SHOELACES AND, WHEN HE HITS THE FLOOR, SHOUTING: "APRIL FOOL'S DAY!" IS ONE WAY TO DO IT. YOU CAN ALSO CELEBRATE THIS IN OTHER WAYS. IN ODESSA, TOWNSFOLK PARADE THEIR HUMOR THROUGH THE STREETS ON APRIL 1ST WITH FLOATS SKEWERING THE LOCAL POLITICIANS. AND EVEN NON-UKRAINIANS HAVE A LAUGH DURING THE FREE POP CONCERT.

Granted, it's difficult to understand humor in another language. Even more so when you don't even know a single word of that language and can't even read its alphabet. You will have to accept that the best jokes may escape you. Those who look carefully, though, will notice enough peculiar curiosities to be thoroughly astonished.

Humorina in Odessa is about everything: flea markets, carnival processions and a free concert in the city square. During the days preceding the procession, local comedians get themselves and the audience warmed up with long monologues about how bad everything is going in this city on the Black Sea. The typical form of humor in Odessa is a kind of black humor in which the comedian also makes himself the butt of the joke.

Although Humorina has become more and more of a public street celebration, the core element is still satire. But, these days the satiric element is accompanied by children and adults with weird ears on their heads for

UKRAINE

Odessa, Ukraine

PARTICIPATE

Participation is welcome. Dress up! Most spectators just wear a funny little hat, but an extravagant outfit will guarantee contact with the locals.

ORIGIN

Why jokes are made in so many countries on April 1st no one really knows. There are some theories, though. One theory to consider: during the Middle Ages, New Year's was celebrated on the 1st of April in many places, including Europe, until Pope Gregory XIII introduced the calendar as we now know it in 1582. There may have been those who disliked the change of New Year's to January and continued celebrating in April. The modern calendar supporters, however, decided to poke some fun at those old-fashioned folks and started playing jokes on them on the 1st of April.

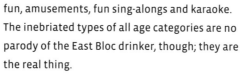

fun, amusements, fun sing-alongs and karaoke. The inebriated types of all age categories are no parody of the East Bloc drinker, though; they are the real thing.

The first Humorina had a noble aim, which was to give the people of Odessa a forum in which to express their frustrations with their politicians – ironically, of course. In 1972, the communist authorities banned the satiric sitcom *KVN*, a popular cult show. The show was aired live a few times, without the possibility of censorship, naturally, and the authorities were not pleased with the anti-Soviet jokes made by the rebellious presenters. In reaction to that prohibition, the *KVN'ers*

organized the day of humor. In three years' time, the festival became so huge that the communists began to fear its influence and yet another ban was enacted. For ten years, Humorina was celebrated indoors, until everyone was eventually allowed to go back in the streets in 1987; the rules had been eased in the spirit of *glasnost*, the government's new attempt at openness.

The celebration reminds us now about the repressive communist period and serves as an opportunity to cope with new adversities such as economic crises, disputes over natural gas, and corrupt politicians. And of course you can also just drink your troubles away at Humorina, too.

🌐 **GUATEMALA**

Antigua, Guatemala.

⚡ **PARTICIPATE**

Everyone can attend the church masses and walk along with the processions.

👍 **TIPS**

Antigua is packed during Semana Santa, so make sure you have arranged a place to stay before you go.

Semana Santa

CATHOLIC WORSHIPPERS IN ANTIGUA, GUATEMALA PRACTICE THEIR RELIGION WITH INCREDIBLE PASSION AND EXUBERANCE. DURING SEMANA SANTA, THEY CARRY DOZENS OF FABULOUS, SPARKLING, SOMETIMES KITSCHY IMAGES OF SAINTS THROUGH THE STREETS ON THEIR SHOULDERS.

APR

THE WEEK PRIOR TO EASTER, USUALLY SOMEWHERE BETWEEN MARCH 23 AND APRIL 22.

You can see an image of a larger-than-life Jesus on the cross being carried on the shoulders of boys and men, dressed in purple habits tied with white waistbands. The men's bodies slowly weave from left to right. You can tell by the looks on their faces that this is not easy work. The float that rests and heaves on their shoulders does not only carry enormous symbolic weight; to the beauty-fully decorated constructions can weigh up to seven thousand pounds.

Every day in Antigua during Semana Santa, the week leading up to Easter, there are solemn ceremonies taking place. On the first day, Palm Sunday, an enormous sculpture of Jesus is taken from its church to be carried through the streets. In addition to Jesus, the statue of Santisima Virgen de Dolores leaves her church to be worshipped by the devout Guatemalans in the open air. After this procession, other sculptures of various saints from different churches follow every day of the

week. Holy fraternities and sisterhoods stand watch the night before over their statues, while copper instruments are played outside.

Along the procession route, residents make *alfombras*, vibrant carpets fashioned from complicated patterns of colored saw-dust that is pressed through cardboard stencils, on the cobblestone streets. The designs of these extraordinary and intricately-designed creations can reflect nature (in particular flowers and vegetables), Biblical themes, and even Mayan traditions. The patterns for the alfombras are often planned months in advance, and it seems a shame that these works of art get trampled by the thousands of worshippers and spectators passing through the streets.

On Good Friday, Antigua is swathed in black; thousands of people crowd the streets, dressed in the color of mourning, burning incense. The most powerful ceremony of the week occurs on this day, on which Jesus' crucifixion is commemorated.

The crucifixion is reenacted by hundreds of worshippers, and the streets are filled with dozens of citizens dressed as Roman soldiers, complete with shields and swords. The image of Jesus on the cross that has been lugged through the streets since daybreak is replaced at noon by a sculpture of a serene Jesus.

On Holy Saturday, there are the funeral processions, followed by processions of women dressed in black to commemorate Mary's suffering in the time after Jesus' crucifixion. And, finally, there is Easter Sunday. Easter is all about rejoicing and celebrating Jesus' resurrection. Fireworks fill the sky, families eat together, and there is partying all day and into the evening.

30

Rouketopolemos

FIFTY THOUSAND ROCKETS WITH LONG WHITE TAILS SLICE THROUGH THE AIR AND LIGHT UP THE NIGHT SKY, BLAZING ACROSS THE TOWN AND ATTEMPTING TO HIT THE OPPOSITE CHURCH'S BELL TOWER. MOST OF THE ROCKETS END UP IN THE NEARBY FOREST, IN THE STREET, OR ON THE ROOFS OF LOCAL RESIDENTS. BUT THOSE ROCKETS THAT END UP – BANG! – HITTING THE OTHER CHURCH'S BELL TOWER SCORE POINTS FOR THEIR TEAM.

Each year at midnight on Easter Sunday in Vrontados, on the Greek island of Chios, the *rouketopolemos*, or rocket war, breaks out. Two church communities (St. Mark's and Panagia Erithiani) aim their homemade rockets at each other's belfries and, when the sun rises, the church that has logged the most hits on its rival is the winner. However, each church invariably declares victory over the other, immediately stating that the actual winner will have to be determined the following year, and thus perpetuating the tradition.

31

👍 TIPS

The best and safest place to view the rocket war is on the slope of Epos, a mountain on the west side of Vrontados.

🌐 GREECE

The town of Vrontados on the Greek island of Chios

⚡ PARTICIPATE

If you are on the island early enough, you may just befriend someone charged with preparing the rockets and lighting them. Perhaps you may also get a chance to set off one of the many fuses. If not, then watching the endless line of thousands of rockets flying through the night is just as exciting.

⬡ ANNO ORIGIN

A struggle between religions, not between churches, is what is believed to have started this rocket extravaganza. When the Islamic Ottoman empire occupied the island, Christians were banned from celebrating Easter, which they had long done . A violent, terrifying rocket war held the occupiers at bay, allowing the Easter celebration to take place.

Months before Easter, the islanders begin their preparations, since fifty thousand rockets can't be assembled in an hour. This event is, naturally, an all-male affair; during the "war," the elderly, women, and children stay inside the two churches that are under siege. There, Easter mass takes place amongst all of the commotion outside, with lovely white candles being lit as a serene counterpoint to the blaring rockets. Villagers have been complaining for years about the festival, because of the hassle the festival creates.

Each year, the homes of the villagers are covered in a fine fireproof metal mesh. But even that doesn't guarantee that a house won't catch fire. "We are trapped in our own tradition," say the old-timers, who no longer find the explosive night so entertaining. But for some, the event never ceases to amaze. The show culminates in the firing of the final rocket, and that kicks off the real party for residents and tourists alike.

32

Kanamara Matsuri

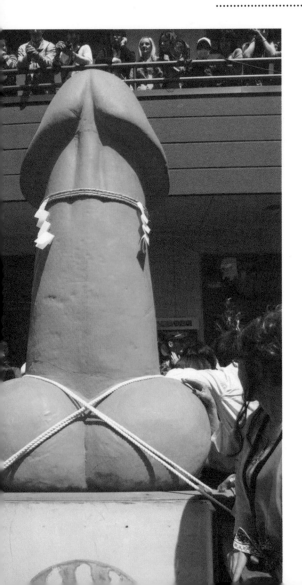

THINK THE JAPANESE ARE SHY, RIGID, AND FRUSTRATED? KANAMARA MATSURI, THE FESTIVAL OF THE STEEL PHALLUS, WILL CHANGE YOUR MIND. SHAMELESSLY, THE LOCALS WILL PUT A PENIS LOLLIPOP IN YOUR MOUTH OR GIVE YOU A LIFE-SIZE VAGINA CANDY.

During this annual Shinto festival, pink penises two and three times the size of the average Japanese person are paraded on mobile altars, called *mikoshi*, through the streets of Kawasaki to the loud cheers of thousands of spectators. All of this penis-worship is a celebration of spring and fertility. The festival has been taking place for hundreds of years. Couples come here from far away to pray for fertility luck. Soon-to-be mothers and fathers pray for a smooth and successful delivery. Prostitutes pray for protection against STDs (that's actually how the whole ritual started, back in the Edo Period). And since a fertile business makes money, business owners even pray to the higher powers for fruitfulness in their professional lives.

As the parade winds through the streets of town, people beat on large, old drums and others dance in ancient masked costumes. It's not at all uncommon to see groups of transvestites holding carrots or radishes carved into penises or grandmothers sucking on penis-shaped lollipops.

Needless to say, there's no shortage of dirty gifts for you to bring back for your friends at home, and plenty of opportunities to have photos taken of you on giant penises made of every conceivable material (wood, metal, sugar, inflatable). Should your appetite be whetted by the parade, you can visit the original steel phallus where it all began or take a tour through the small fertility museum. And a Japanese party is obviously not complete without karaoke. *"Don't want no short dick man!"*

APR

ANNUALLY, USUALLY ON THE FIRST SUNDAY OF APRIL, DURING THE TWO-WEEK CHERRY BLOSSOM SEASON.

JAPAN

Kawasaki, Japan.

PARTICIPATE

Watch the parade, take some pictures with dicks, buy obscene sweets.

ORIGIN

The legend goes that a young girl had a demon inside her vagina which castrated two men she slept with. Logical that no man wanted to be with her after that. Desperate, she sought help from a blacksmith, who made her an iron penis to use to fool the demon. The ruse worked: the demon bit his teeth on it. The black-smith was honored with his own altar in Kawasaki -in the shape of a penis, obviously. Around 1800, the prostitutes of the city began to make pilgrimages to the altar, seeking protection against syphilis and praying for busy nights. The fertility festival in Kawasaki is now the largest in Japan.

Thunder over Louisville

THE EARTH THUNDERS UNDER YOUR FEET, EXPLOSIONS RATTLE YOUR BELLY AND THE LIGHT SHOW BLINDS YOUR EYES. YEAH! THUNDER OVER LOUISVILLE IS OVER THE TOP IN EVERY WAY – A GIGANTIC FIREWORKS SHOW THAT LASTS ALMOST A HALF HOUR, OVERWHELMING SPECTATORS, IN TRUE AMERICAN STYLE.

Have you maybe seen a few fireworks lighting up the sky on New Year's Eve or on Bastille Day in France? That's child's play compared to this pyrotechnical extravaganza. Tons of fireworks – both graceful and jarring – shoot up in the sky above Louisville, Kentucky. The show is carefully choreographed and unfolds to a specially created soundtrack. The show is different every year, but it always contains 'Thunder's signature one-mile waterfall', which seems to rain down from the Second Street Bridge. This breathtaking signature effect is the highlight of the event, the mile-long blaze lasting for minutes and not only lighting up the whole bridge but also the Ohio River below.

 ORIGIN

The Kentucky Derry Festival
has been celebrated since
the 1950s. At the end of
the 1980s, the Louisville
residents thought an official
opening ceremony was
called for. The first firework
show was held in 1990, but
compared to the current
spectacle, the original had
more of an amateur feel.

👍 **TIPS**

⚡ Check the site **thun-deroverlouisville.org** for advice on where to park. You will also have to lock up your bike, because biking and skating is forbidden on the riverbanks.

⚡ Pre-game drinking is recommended since bringing your own alcohol is forbidden on the shores. You will be checked, but plastic bottles are allowed. The only place to get beer is Waterfront Park.

More than half a million spectators annually attend this dazzling display, the opening ceremony of the Kentucky Derby Festival - a two week medley of sports events, including a marathon, that celebrates the famous Kentucky Derby. Waterfront Park in Louisville is the most popular spot for watching the fireworks. There you can listen to the music and find food stands and the occasional bar that serves beer. Considering that the fireworks are lit from big pontoons in the middle of the river, the view is just as good from either side. It's worth nothing that the Ohio River also functions as the state border, on the opposite side from Louisville you'll find Jeffersonville, located in the state of Indiana.

Those thrill-seekers who come to experience the evening's explosion of colors will need to claim their spots early in the day. Everyone wants the best position to plant his or her lawn chair, and this creates a traffic jam hours in advance. Either way, you will have to walk the last mile to the park. For some that is quite a lot.

To entertain the waiting crowd, some airplanes were called in a couple of years ago, and this diversion has since grown into the Thunder Air Show – "one of the top five in the country!!", according to the organizers. Over a hundred planes perform their acrobatic tricks above the water and the bridges. Among them are old airplanes as well as the newest models from the American army. The air show starts at 3 pm and lasts until 9 pm. Around that time, the excitement on the shores reaches its climax. Patriotic songs *(The Star Spangled Banner, America the Beautiful)* reverberate through the speakers, and at 9:30 sharp the firework artists press their buttons.

Bam! Phhheeeeeeew! Oooooh! Aaaaaah!

33

Songkran

A SPLASH OF COLD WATER ON YOUR BACK IS ESPECIALLY REFRESHING WHEN IT'S 35 DEGREES. THEN, AS YOU TURN AROUND, YOU CATCH A GLIMPSE OF THE THAI TEENAGERS HIGH FIVING EACH OTHER AT YOUR EXPENSE. NOTHING BEATS A RICH, WET TOURIST. THAT IS, OF COURSE, UNLESS THAT TOURIST IS A WOMAN, AND SHE HAS A SEE-THROUGH SHIRT ON.

Songkran is the Thai new year and it means three days of craziness. Craziness with water and white lime powder. Nowhere in Thailand are you safe. Cities, villages, squares, even backstreets ... once you put one foot outside, there is someone ready to spray you down, pour a bucket of water over you from a first floor window, or wipe white powder in your face. Whole battalions of Songkran residents drive pickups through the streets, each carrying a ton of water.

Many city dwellers return to their small hometowns to celebrate Songkran with their families. In the morning, it's off to the temple to honor their ancestors. The Thai youth lightly sprinkle water on the hands of the elderly to show their respect, images of Buddha are carefully washed, and houses are thoroughly cleaned.

The water-throwing is not only for fun, but also symbolizes the cleansing of one's spirit. The tradition began when the water from large Buddha statues trickled down onto the elderly who were worshipping below.

If a whole bucket is poured over you, just think – all your sins have been washed away – letting you begin the new year free of all transgressions.

34

🌐 THAILAND

In Thailand and Laos

⚜ ORIGIN

The word Songkran comes from the Sanskrit word "to move" or "to change place". On this particular occasion, it represents the sun's movement and marks the beginning of a new year.

👍 TIPS

⚡ Being out in the streets means lots of water and getting soaked to the bone. So if you are taking important items with you, like your passport, be sure to place them in a water-tight bag or container; better yet, bring a copy of your passport instead.

⚡ Women who do not want to have extra water thrown on them and be groped by the enthusiastic men are advised not to wear white shirts.

⚡ PARTICIPATE

If you're in Thailand or Laos during Songkran, then not participating is only an option if you stay inside all day. If you decide to venture outside, you are then presented with two options: Become a victim or strike back hard. The latter is clearly more fun. So grab your Super Soakers, water balloons, buckets, and plastic bottles and soak everything and everyone in your path.

35
Naghol

Since 1463

JUST ONE LOOK AT THESE HARDCORE BUNGEE JUMPERS WILL GIVE YOU A BIGGER ADRENALINE RUSH THAN STANDING ON THE EDGE OF A BRIDGE ABOUT TO ATTEMPT YOUR OWN BUNGEE JUMP. THE LIVES OF THE MEN ON PENTECOST ISLAND, IN VANUATU, DEPEND ON THE VINES THAT ARE TIED AROUND THEIR ANKLES. AND SOMETIMES THE VINES BREAK.

Every now and then a jumper breaks a hip, a back, a leg, or worse. The men do not jump to have a cool story to tell or because they have lost a bet, but to secure the coming year's yam harvest. The greater the distance of the jump, the higher the crops will grow, it is said. And it will not suffice for a diver to just dangle above the ground, since the goal is for each diver – his head tucked into his shoulders – to brush his shoulders against the ground. Peer pressure, in addition to the burden of ensuring next year's harvest, can also provide a needed boost of courage.

Naghol or *land diving* has been done here for hundreds of years. The towers the men dive from are built from wood that is freshly cut, to make sure it is strong. These towers can be 20 or 30 meters high, with the lowest diving platform (for young boys) at 10 meters. The vines are also fresh from the forest, and need to be elastic and full of sap. Each jumper gets his own vines, the length appropriate to his weight and height of his jump. As the women sing and stomp their feet harder and faster on the muddy ground, the jumper on the tower takes one more deep breath.

Today's bungee jumpers know (almost) for sure that nothing will go wrong, but the land divers have no such consolation. Things very often go terribly wrong since there is no safety equipment and the vines are sometimes poorly chosen. As you might expect, there are frequent injuries and there has been at least one reported death. When Queen Elizabeth II visited the island in 1974, the

VANUATU

ORIGIN

In villages in the south of Pentecost Island, Republic of Vanuatu.

Nobody knows for sure, but naturally there's a nice story attached to the ritual. A woman, Tamalie, was so unhappy with the sexual demands of her husband that she ran away to the forest. Her husband followed her, so she climbed a banyan tree. After her husband climbed up after her, she tied vines to her ankles, jumped off the tree and survived. Her husband jumped after her without tying vines to his ankles and died. It is said that the island men now perform the ritual to ensure that they will not be fooled again.

islanders staged a Naghol show for her benefit. Unfortunately, the vines were too dry (it was not the right season for land diving, but how often does a reigning British monarch visit?), and someone died in the ritual.

Between April and June, land dives take place across the island since the ritual has become a profitable tourist income for the local people. Indeed, the more they jump, the more prosperity they secure – after all, just to watch, each tourist pays 100 euros.

PENTECOST ISLAND

REPUBLIC VANUATU

Afrika Burn

FREE SPIRITS, UNITE! BLACK OR WHITE, MALE OR FEMALE,
DRESSED OR NAKED... COME GATHER IN THE SOUTH AFRICAN
DESERT, LEAVE YOUR INHIBITIONS BEHIND IN THE CAR, AND
FOLLOW YOUR DESIRE TO THE AFRIKA BURN FESTIVAL.

Haters will call this a total rip-off of Burning Man (see p.84). Which it is. In fact, it's almost an exact replica of the American desert festival in which everything is about gifting and radical self-expression. But who cares? This is, after all, about positivity, and who can have a problem with that? The first African version was organized in 2007, at that time going by the name of Afrika Burns.

But that name was deemed too controversial in a country that was, and still is, often ablaze due to racial riots. The name was later changed to Africa Burn, and it has stayed that way. Just like the American flagship, Afrika Burn sets up its tents in an isolated desert location, in this case it's the nature park called Tankwa Karoo, a three and a half hour drive north of Cape Town. There,

(see p.84)

SOUTH AFRICA

Tankwa Karoo, South Africa.

TIPS

You have to buy a ticket to get in.
Check: www.afrikaburn.com for more info.

PARTICIPATE

Not participating is not an option. As soon as you walk through the gate, you are considered to be a piece of art yourself, so you'd better behave like one. And don't forget to take something to contribute to the gifting economy. Condoms, beads, lollipops, pills, a kit for makeup sessions, anything goes.
- Create an artistic installation
- Construct a theme camp with your friends
- Offer a service
- Turn your body into a piece of art
- Paint your chassis
- Build a stage and give a performance
- Build an artistic vehicle
- Become a volunteer

on a desert plain, the San Clan is built. This is a towering structure that goes up in flames at the end of the festival, just like The Man at Burning Man in America. The San Clan sculpture is supposed to resemble a caveman's drawing of a bunch of people. A happy bunch of people, of course. Specifically, a happy, partying bunch of people, because Afrika Burn is all about creating a jovial community, or so the organization says.

There are no big sponsors, and therefore no publicity. Nothing can be bought at the festival, and nothing is allowed to be sold. You will have to bring all the food and drinks that you will need for the six days, and bringing five liters of water is obligatory. You'll get some other stuff through gifting - the economy of giving without expecting something in return. There is also a name for the political system of the festival, *do-ocracy*. It means that if you think something should be or should have been done at Afrika Burn, you should feel free to do it yourself. The community does not want observers, only participants.

Art is the most important source of entertainment. You'll encounter bizarre constructions, beautiful statues, interactive installations, and much more. Body art is also encouraged. But you can always just do something small like paint some jewelry, or, even more simple, make some drawings. You can set up your own little themed camp. A Post Office, for example, and then you can go deliver postcards at the festival grounds. Or perhaps your own club, massage parlor, or center with workshops for nude painting, Bikram yoga, or welding. The purpose is for each person to let go and reveal his true self. Relaxed and free.

Chat with everyone about whatever you feel like, dance deliriously, even if no one else is dancing, or roll over in the sand like a dog. The fact that all this free expression tends to result in, um, full exposure, is indicated in a small line on the festival's website: 'the welcoming committee is looking forward to meet you at the entrance, sometimes wearing only a smile and nothing else'. But no worries, it's not necessary to go commando. You can always keep your clothes on if you prefer.

36

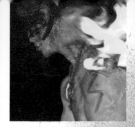

Beltane

HUNDREDS OF HALF-NAKED WOMEN, THEIR BODIES PAINTED,
RUN AROUND ECSTATICALLY IN THE DARK, ILLUMINATED BY
TORCHES AND FIRES. THIS CAN ONLY MEAN ONE THING:
FERTILITY! SPRING! BELTANE!

On this day, according to pre-Christian beliefs, Mother Nature opens up to the fertility god and this union results in new crops and new life. To honor this occasion, dozens of musicians and performers wearing little more than body paint and carrying massive torches parade through Edinburgh.

The Beltane festival is a beautiful, magical spectacle. It's startling to see how, in this far corner of modern Europe, hundreds of volunteers have cobbled together a potpourri of ancient spring and fertility celebrations into one festival and executed this event to perfection. If not for a few modern giveaways here and there, you would think, while watching this procession, that you had been transported back fifteen hundred years in time.

It's surprising that the festival in its present form has only been in existence since 1988. For decades, Scots built a fire here and there to celebrate Beltane, but that was really it. But then a handful of enthusiasts decided to return to their Celtic roots and created the Beltane festival, copying the ancient rituals as much as possible while still adding in some of their own touches. These days, thousands of visitors flock to this exceptional event and tickets are always sold out for the site. Hundreds of volunteers are involved in the creation of the costumes, torches, face and body painting, and the intricate choreography of the procession. The fire costs the Beltane Fire Society, which runs the festival, five thousand pounds per event. Well, there's the modern age for you.

37

SCOTLAND

Calton Hill in Edinburgh, Scotland.

....

ORIGIN

The word Beltane probably derives from a Gaelic-Celtic word that means bright, sacred fire. Before use of the twelve-month Roman calendar, the Celts divided the year into four periods, each celebrated with its own day. Beltane heralded the coming of spring and was observed on the day of the full moon during the time when the hawthorns were blooming and cattle were sent to the pasture. On this night, everyone left their huts on the plains or in the mountains to come together for a fire ceremony, complete with sacrifices, intended to drive out evil and encourage fertility.

....

TIPS

There are only about twelve thousand tickets sold for the festival, and it's always sold out. For information on tickets, visit **www.beltane.org.**

....

ON THE NIGHT OF APRIL 30 TO MAY 1.

38 Queensday

THE DUTCH STILL REMAIN MERCHANTS AT HEART. EVEN IF HE'S WEARING AN ORANGE INFLATABLE CROWN OVER AN ORANGE WIG WHILE DRINKING A HEINEKEN, A DUTCHMAN IS INTERESTED IN MAKING MONEY. INDEED, QUEENSDAY IS ALL ABOUT TRADING WITH A DRINK IN YOUR HAND.

Of course you can always just join the partying masses on Dam Square or Museum Square; but, to be honest, you can also do that for pretty much any other holiday or celebration. The *real* Queensday can be found away from the mobs of tourists, since the real way the Dutch honor their queen is by doing a royal amount of drinking and striking bargains.

By sunrise, the youngest entrepreneurs have already set up their stalls in the city's main park, the Vondelpark. If you decide to stroll through there in the morning, you'll be bombarded by children wanting to perform for you – playing a fiddle, acting out a play, singing a song, doing some gymnastics – for a few cents, of course. The adults get in on the action, too, dragging boxes of their unwanted possessions to a specific spot on the pavement that they've reserved long in advance. Others try to make a bit of money by doing creative acts: you might see a group dressed as a 'living fruit machine', or someone else dressed as the Queen and offering photo ops (for a fee, naturally). It may not sound like a party to most people, but for the Dutch, the

 NETHERLANDS

Amsterdam, the Netherlands.

 PARTICIPATE

 ORIGIN

Queensday has been celebrated since 1890, although when it began it was just a normal holiday on August 31. After the coronation of Queen Juliana in 1949, the celebration was moved to her birthday, April 30. Upon her coronation in 1980, Queen Beatrix decided not to change the date, even though her birthday is January 31. The birthday of her heir, Willem-Alexander, is on April 27, so it's likely that the holiday will remain on April 30.

- Do like the locals do: wear orange and stroll around the flea market looking for bargains. Drink a Heineken, do some tequila shots, and dance along the canals.
- Book a boat or a spot on a boat ahead of time and sail slowly through the crowded canals. Loud music on the boats is now prohibited.
- Make yourself some money. Come up with an inventive act or just try to sell some of your stuff.

clatter of another euro in the bread box, combined with a pulsating beat and lots of drinks with friends, is pure bliss. Plus, the boost you get from scoring a brand-new secondhand dress for only five euros is one that lasts all day. Around noon, the day's trading completed, the Dutch can begin to really focus on partying. The bottles of vodka come out. Space Brownies replace the apple pies on offer earlier in the day.

People immediately spend all the money they earned in the morning at one of the many outside bars or at one of the huge outdoor parties. Roam the city, dance, jump on one of the party boats filling the canals, smoke, and flirt all day until the city sends out the crews to clean the streets of all the empty beer cans and orange paraphernalia. One day a year, orange is indeed the most beautiful color in the world!

Lotus Lantern Festival

A CHARMING SMILE, ILLUMINATED BY THOUSANDS OF LANTERNS. THE LOTUS LANTERN FESTIVAL IN SEOUL IS FILLED WITH LIGHTS, COLORS, DANCES, AND ENDLESSLY FALLING FLOWER PETALS.

Korean Buddhists put on their finest clothes for this event, which commemorates Buddha's birthday. For Buddhists, the lighting of lotus-shaped lanterns symbolizes the brightening up of the dark places on earth where there is pain and suffering. The highlight of this festival is undoubtedly the lantern parade, which features more than 100,000 enormous, illuminated lotus flowers, pagodas, dragons, and other types of lanterns. The parade is held on the Sunday before Buddha's birthday, in the beginning of May. For several days prior to the parade, people make elaborate preparations and the city has a festive feeling. Stands alongside the road display the traditional lanterns – in the shapes of animals, plants and images of rural life. There are tea ceremonies and dance demonstrations, and monks invite people to join them in meditation. The parade starts on Sunday at seven in the evening. All shapes, forms and colors of lanterns pass by. It takes over three hours for the hundreds of thousands of lanterns to make their way along the parade route.

When the lantern procession reaches its destination, Jogyesa Temple, a huge shower of flower petals rains down upon the revelers from the night sky. You'll see thousands of ecstatic, smiling faces delighting in the scented

🌐 SOUTH KOREA

Seoul, South Korea.

◆ ORIGIN

For over six hundred years, the Buddhists of Seoul have been celebrating Buddha's birthday with lanterns. The lighting of a lotus-shaped lantern traditionally symbolized religious devotion, doing good deeds, and bringing light to the dark corners of the earth and into the hearts of the people. These days, the city of Seoul promotes the festival as a multicultural party for people of all religions, races, and backgrounds.

rain. Dance groups perform their choreographies on the swelling petal stage. And, as ten thousand lanterns carrying wishes are launched into the sky, everyone dances until the floating lights are completely out of sight.

39

40

Cheung Chau Bun

SCALING A TOWER OF SWEET BUNS IS NOT TOO TOUGH. BUT THE DIFFICULTY INCREASES WHEN YOU KNOW THAT GRABBING THE HIGHEST BUN WILL BRING THE MOST HAPPINESS IN THE FUTURE. SO YOU CAN IMAGINE THE COMPETITION BETWEEN THE CLIMBERS IS FIERCE.

In the late 1970s, one of the high towers collapsed under the weight of all the climbers and over one hundred people were injured. So these days the competition no longer features actual sweet buns but rather plastic ones, which make the tower less slippery. However, you can still see towers built in the original manner – bamboo structures covered with actual sweet buns – all over the island of Cheung Chau during the annual Bun Festival. Some of the highest and most elaborate towers are made from steel frames instead of bamboo and contain more than eight thousand steamed buns. The buns are usually filled with lotus seed paste, sesame, or red beans.

The race to the top of the bun tower is the highlight of this merry week of Chinese parades, delicious (vegetarian) food, and opera and dance performances on Cheung Chau, ten kilometers southwest of Hong Kong. There's live music and the streets are filled with nicely dressed – and sometimes costumed – locals enjoying the festive atmosphere. On the day of the bun race, a colorful and whimsical procession, headed by a picture of Pak Tai, the water god, winds through the streets. Drummers beat their hardest to dispel the evil spirits, and then the frantic and bizarre race to the top of the bun tower takes place. If you feel like bringing some of the good vibes of the festival home with you, pick up a plastic bun souvenir or two.

MAY

THE EIGHTH DAY OF THE FOURTH MOON IN THE CHINESE CALENDAR, USUALLY IN MAY.

CHEUNG CHAU
長洲

Reservoir
配水庫

Tung Wan Beach
東灣海灘

Kwun Yam Wan
觀音灣

Central

Warwick Hotel
長洲華威酒店

Wai San Back Street

Peak Road

Can't go a day without meat? You'll have to smuggle in beef jerky from the mainland. During the Bread Festival, the whole island is vegetarian. Even McDonald's adapts to the regimen — no hamburgers, only mushroom burgers.

HONG KONG

Cheung Chau, Hong Kong.

ORIGIN

In the 18th century, there was a terrible plague that killed a large portion of the islanders. When the plague ended, the religiously-minded locals organized a Taoist bun festival to thank their gods.

TIPS

Bun Bang Fai is celebrated throughout northeastern Thailand and Laos, although it does not always happen on the same weekend in each place.

🌐 BOLIVIA

The biggest Tinku is organized in the village of Macha during the first week of May. Other villages where Tinkus are organized include Sacaca and Torotoro. These are all in the same region of Potosí, Bolivia.

....

🏅 ORIGIN

Tinkus have likely been organized since 1100, as sacrifices to Pachamama, Mother Nature. If someone lost his life in the fighting, it was considered the ultimate sacrifice that would bring forth new life and fertility. The Catholic Church has long strived to ban Tinku and still discourages the fighting.

....

⚡ PARTICIPATE

If you don't intend to participate in the fighting, keep your distance and observe. There's a steady flow of alcohol and the atmosphere can suddenly change from festive to more dangerous. The police, not necessarily sober themselves, can interfere quite brutally with batons or tear gas. Make sure you're more sober than the locals so you can anticipate a change in atmosphere at all times and make your getaway if things get really heated.

The villages where the Tinkus are held are truly tiny. No luxury hotels here - not even multiple-room hostels. Make sure you reserve a room well in advance with a local or ask a guide to do that for you.

....

Tinku

THE MORE BLOOD, THE BETTER. SO, THE BOLIVIANS AIM THEIR FISTS AT EACH OTHER'S NOSES. SOME MEN WILL EVEN WRAP STRIPS OF CLOTH STUDDED WITH SHARDS OF GLASS TO THEIR WRISTS TO ATTACK WITH. THE BLOODSTAINS IN THE DUSTY STREETS ARE CONSIDERED A SACRIFICE TO MOTHER NATURE, AND ONLY THROUGH THE SPILLING OF SOME BLOOD CAN A PROSPEROUS AND FERTILE NEW YEAR BE SECURED.

This ritual is all about the prosperity of the community, Bolivians from the poor region of Potosí say. The barren highlands of this area yield very little food, and the peasants believe that if they don't get a higher power on their side even the potato harvest will fail and there will be nothing at all to eat. Through the ritual of Tinku, they work to ensure a fruitful harvest.

Tinkus, meaning 'meetings' in the local language, are today only held in the region of Potosí. The different communities gather in the sandy streets of a few small villages that contain little but thin mountain air. If they're available, the best outfits emerge from the closet for three days of intense fighting and drinking. You'll see vibrantly colored belts and scarves, neatly knitted woolen socks, accented with neon green and neon pink. Many of the fighters wear a leather helmet similar to those of the Conquistadors, the Spanish soldiers who, centuries ago, brought the native population of this land to its knees.

In the streets, villagers drink *chicha* (a drink made from maize) and dance. Some men will then form a circle, and while the circle is still dancing around them, two men in the middle will start throwing some punches, preferably until blood starts to flow. After those two men, another pair will take the spot in the middle, and so on. All the while, the men forming the circle are egging on the fighters. Sometimes the fighters need to be pulled apart, and it wouldn't be the first time that things have gotten a bit out of control.

In theory, Tinkus are organized for the physical and spiritual benefit of the whole community. But even the importance of the ritual cannot necessarily prevent the event from degenerating into one huge fistfight. People have died during these fights, mostly because fighters were arming themselves with more and more weapons. Nowadays, the police are there to supervise and to make sure only blood comes out of the bodies, no last breaths. The police also check the combatants for glass, bludgeons and guns. On top of that, the authorities are also there to verify what might be the cause of spectators passing out in the streets – too much excitement, the sight of blood or perhaps an excess of alcohol?

Young women also wage war against one another, in similar circles. Giggles turn into vicious smacks, long black braids flying through the air. A referee is there to split up the ladies, if it comes to that. Naturally, even when fighting, the young women keep one eye on the guys to check out who fights the hardest and with the most style, and who's best at fielding the incoming punches. Because when it comes down to flirting and hooking up, Tinku is not too different from any other party.

41

Waisak

42

BOROBUDUR IS WITHOUT DOUBT ONE OF THE MOST IMPRESSIVE TEMPLES IN INDONESIA. THE TROPICAL HEAT COMBINES WITH THE ANCIENT, HOLY SURROUNDINGS GIVES THIS PLACE A MYSTICAL FEELING. ADD TO THIS THE SOUND OF HUNDREDS OF MONKS SINGING ON *VESAKHA PUJA* AND EVEN A NON-BELIEVER MIGHT BE CONVERTED.

Long before sunrise, the monks come shuffling to the temple, barefoot and dressed in their orange habits. In lotus position they pray, chant and sing, hundreds of voices together. One monk may whisper, another may sing loudly. If you sit down and close your eyes, you can be transported on the waves of the mantras, inhaling the thick tropical air and waiting until the sunrise slowly illuminates the most important Buddhist temple in Indonesia.

On Vesakha Puja, also known as Waisak, Buddhists celebrate Buddha's birth, his enlightenment, and his death. Believers celebrate the holy day with extra offerings of flowers, candles, and incense. They also pray and are expected to behave more devoutly by, for instance, not eating any meat and making themselves useful in the community. It's common to see many people going to the temples, cleaning, helping the poor, and giving the monks something extra to eat.

In Indonesia, Vesakha Puja is a national holiday, to allow Buddhists from

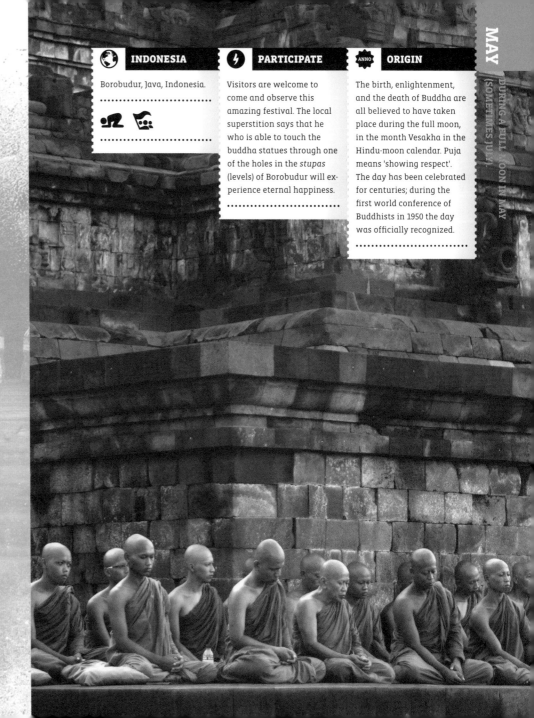

INDONESIA

Borobudur, Java, Indonesia.

PARTICIPATE

Visitors are welcome to come and observe this amazing festival. The local superstition says that he who is able to touch the buddha statues through one of the holes in the *stupas* (levels) of Borobudur will experience eternal happiness.

ORIGIN

The birth, enlightenment, and the death of Buddha are all believed to have taken place during the full moon, in the month Vesakha in the Hindu-moon calendar. Puja means 'showing respect'. The day has been celebrated for centuries; during the first world conference of Buddhists in 1950 the day was officially recognized.

all over the country to make the pilgrimage to Borobudur. Every year, hundreds of monks and over ten thousand of the Buddhist faithful make the trek to the famed temple on Java. Throughout the day, throngs of people come and go. A horn sounds out low, melancholy notes and the drums set the pace. In the morning and evening there are processions from Mendut temple, where one of the biggest Buddha statues is located, to Borobudur, a few kilometers away. Here and there, you can see both party tents and rugs for praying. Religious celebrants set down their offerings in the temple and then fold their hands. They also climb up the temple, which is a symbol for the cosmos. They must start at the bottom level, the symbol of earthly life, and ascend all the way up to the highest *stupa*, which symbolizes nirvana. Having reached nirvana, they must then go back down to earth again.

Bun Bang Fai

BAMBOO STICKS, PVC, LOTS OF GUNPOWDER, ALL TIED TOGETHER WITH VINES AND LIT WITH A FUSE. THE LAO PEOPLE LAUNCH THEIR HOME-MADE MISSILES INTO THE SKY TO ASK THE GODS FOR A FERTILE RAINY SEASON.

The Thai are known for their smiles, but their giggles are even better. They also have quite a bawdy sense of humor, and with rockets the theme for this festival, you can imagine they have a great time. The festival is celebrated only in the northeastern of Thailand and Laos – the ethnic Lao people share a heritage that transcends the border.

There are rocket-filled celebrations in many villages throughout the region, but the most impressive spectacle takes place in Yasothon, the capital of the northeast Thai province. There, you can enjoy three days of dance processions, parades, heavy drinking, and the much-anticipated rocket extravaganza. There are a lot of beers available over the counter, but the most popular drink is what they call Lao Whiskey, which is made from corn and blessed with the perfect combination of a high alcohol content and a low price. That's why almost everyone, including the elderly, gets incredibly drunk during this celebration.

The drinking and giggling begins on Friday. On Sat-

urday, there are a number of parades with elaborate floats, many of which feature phallic symbols and imagery (a nod to the tradition's origins as a fertility ritual). Cross-dressing, both cross-sex and cross-generational, is also a part of the festivities. And on this day, of course, the all-important rockets are paraded through the streets. These range from small rockets to nine-foot whoppers and are beautiful to look at, with intricate wood carvings and renderings of heads of *nagas*, the mythical snake of the Mekong. They are carried around on beautiful colored platforms by men in brightly colored attire.

Sunday is time for the climax. The missiles are raised up on high towers and launched, to much cheering. In the rocketcompetition, points are awarded for the look of the weapon, the elegance of the trail it leaves in the air, and, above all, the distance it travels. Those whose rockets don't travel far can get muddy. But that's really no big deal, since almost everyone jumps into the mud at some point anyway.

🌐 THAILAND

Yasothon, northeastern
Thailand.

👍 TIPS

Bun Bang Fai is celebrated
throughout northeastern
Thailand and Laos, although
it does not always happen
on the same weekend in
each place. In the capital of
Laos, Vientiane, the festival
is also celebrated.

⚙ ORIGIN

According to the legend,
there was once a god of rain
called Vassakan. He loved
to be worshipped with fire,
and the villagers strived
to please him to ensure a
heavy rain and a bountiful
harvest. So, with great difficulty, they cobbled together
a rocket, a Bang Fai, and
they launched it up to Vassakan in heaven. And sure
enough, after all this effort,
the rain began.

44 Cheese Rolling

THE CHEESE HURTLES DOWN THE STEEP, ROCKY HILL WITH THE PARTICIPANTS CHASING WILDLY AFTER IT, UNAFRAID OF THE POTENTIAL BROKEN ANKLES AND NOSES THAT MIGHT RESULT. WELCOME TO THE ANNUAL COOPER'S HILL CHEESE ROLLING.

The people of Brockworth, a town in the Cotswolds region of England, have been participating in this event for over 200 years. The cheese of choice is a hard Double Gloucester that is made locally. The winner is the first man to cross the finish line after the cheese. This quaint local tradition has, over the years, grown into an incredibly popular event. It now attracts visitors – thousands of them – from far outside the village limits. In fact, over the last five years, so many people have shown up that crowd control and ensuring adequate medical treatment for the injured became major issues. In 2010, the event was banned by the British health services due to safety concerns.

Yet, even though the official event was canceled, there was still an informal event held and 500 crazy souls barreled down the hill; needless to say, not all of them made it to the bottom with their ankles intact.

But, fear not, the festival is now 'officially' organized, with permits, rules, gates, proper crowd control features, and enough rescuers and ambulances on hand. But regardless of permits or licenses, undertaking this bumpy, risky free fall behind the cheese remains a slightly mad endeavor. If you're lucky, there might be a friendly volunteer at the bottom of the hill who will kindly tend to your broken bones. And then you can always retire to The Cheese Rollers, a nearby pub, to drink away your aches and pains and revel in your heroics.

Between 1941 and 1954, when food was in short supply, the cheese was replaced by a wooden lookalike – a tiny block of cheese was hidden in the middle of it.

BROCKWORTH

ENGLAND

Cooper's Hill, Brockworth,
England.

ORIGIN

Cheese Rolling has been a
tradition here for over 200
years, but how it started
is unclear. One theory attributes it to the Romans,
since they were appar-
ently quite fond of throwing
things down hills and running after them.

TIPS

Do not start too early. The
countdown to the start of
the race goes like this:
- **one** to be ready
- **two** to be steady
- **three** to prepare... (at
  that time the cheese is
  released)
And at...
- **four** to be off

PARTICIPATE

Until 2010, all you needed
to do was simply report at
the top of the hill on the day
of the event, but this may
change due to the new safety measures. Before you go,
make sure to check **www.
cheeserolling.co.uk**. There
are five downhill races (including one for women), and
four uphill ones for boys
and girls under 12. Winners
receive ten pounds and the
cheese.

El Colacho

THE DEVIL, WEARING NIKES, LEAPS INTO THE AIR, BOUNDING OVER MATTRESSES COVERED WITH ROWS OF SWEET LITTLE BABIES. THE BELIEF IS THAT, AS THE DEVIL REPRESENTATIVE LEAPS OVER THE BABIES, HE WILL TAKE ALL THEIR EVIL WITH HIM AND CLEANSE THE NEWBORNS OF ORIGINAL SIN.

El Salto del Colacho (the Jump of the Devil) has been taking place in Castrillo de Murcia, Spain since 1620. It's a bit like a steeplechase: the Colacho, or Devil, makes his way down a long, winding street dotted with a number of mattresses containing dozens of babies (all born in the past year) in their finest lace outfits. The Devil takes a running start, jumps the mattress, runs, changes direction, jumps another mattress, runs, and so on - all accompanied by the screams and, hopefully, sighs of relief, of the anxious parents and other onlookers.

While the ritual's origins are not entirely clear, it seems, like so many Spanish traditions, to be a blend of folklore and Catholicism. After all, this baby jumping event is an element (arguably the strangest, and certainly the most

45

EVERY YEAR ON THE SUNDAY FOLLOWING THE CATHOLIC FEAST OF CORPUS CHRISTI, USUALLY EARLY JUNE.

SPAIN

Castrillo de Murcia, near Burgos, Spain.

ORIGIN

The likely origin of the baby jumping tradition is a pagan ritual. As with many pagan celebrations and traditions, the Catholic Church essentially took the existing tradition, annexed a saint to it, and transformed it into a Christian celebration.

PARTICIPATE

If you really want to have an exciting time at this event, bring your own baby and place him or her on the street with the others. The Devil is also fine with jumping over babies that are not from Castrillo de Murcia.

Since
1620

dangerous, element) of the Catholic festival of Corpus Christi, which is celebrated throughout Spain. For days in advance of the jumping, there are processions and masses and popular celebrations, culminating with the jumping that takes place after mass on Sunday. If the Devil manages to clear all the hurdles, he is chased from the village, not to come back for another year. Once the Devil has left town, people can relax and really begin drinking.

Stinging Nettle Eating Championship

46

ROLLING UP THE STINGING NETTLE LEAF BEFORE YOU EAT IT SEEMS TO LIMIT THE PAIN, BUT ANYONE WHO EATS SO MANY OF THESE LONG, RAW, SPINY BLADES WITHIN AN HOUR IS GOING TO FEEL IT IN THE END.

The competition focuses on eating the leaves off the nettle stalks and seeing how many you can completely clear through. The branches are carefully measured in two-foot lengths. During the period of an hour, competitors consume as many of the branches and their leaves as possible. Past champions have eaten over seventy feet's worth of nettles, but the length is not everything. One year, there may be a better crop than the previous year, meaning more leaves and more spiny bits that have to be cleared away. This is no easy task, especially since the nettles puncture your gums, lips, tongue and throat.

The nettles, which some say taste like raw beans, are difficult to chew. Fortunately, beer and water are allowed - and some participants will even dip the leaves in the beer before placing them on their tongues. Then there is the matter of digestion. As the leaves begin to rapidly ferment in the stomach, the bubbling sound that results is a bit like the sound sheep make while eating. This noise causes many participants to give back their chewed leaves while the race is still in progress. Dozens of people participate each year, men and women alike, and all end up with black tongues. The participants all sit at beer tables on a large

stage, allowing the audience a great view of their pained faces. The pub that has been organizing the event since 1996, The Bottle Inn, offers an entire weekend of fun, with a barbeque to remove the bad nettle taste, entertainment for kids, and plenty of beer. Just for fun, nettle beer is also available. The nettles used come from the area around the pub and are cut just hours before the event. If they're not fresh, they don't sting. And that would be a shame.

ENGLAND

The Bottle Inn, Marshwood, England

PARTICIPATE

This competition is about persistence, pacing yourself, and the willpower to ignore the pain and suppress your gag reflex - petal by petal, stem by stem. Mercifully, you are allowed to give up halfway through. If you choose to participate, the jury is strict - they watch for people throwing away leaves and for those who have tried to bring their own stems to place on the pile. Nothing goes unnoticed. Vomiting afterwards is permitted.
Visit **www. bottleinn.co.uk** for dates and times.

ORIGIN

As much nonsense does, this began with a bet, the winner being the person with the longest nettles on his land. Farmer Alex Williams was absolutely certain that he had the longest, with just over fifteen feet. He boasted to anyone who could bring a longer nettle that he would eat that nettle. Naturally, someone produced a longer nettle, and Williams ate the entire thing, to the great amusement of the rest of the patrons of The Bottle Inn. That was in 1986. When a new owner bought the pub the next year and wanted to organize something fun, he organized a stinging nettle race against the already-legendary local, Alex Williams. And so the madness began.

47 Santo António

THE PORTUGUESE ARE FOND OF SAINTS, AND THE BIRTHDAY OF AN IMPORTANT SAINT MEANS PARTY TIME. SO YOU CAN IMAGINE THAT THE BIRTHDAY OF SAN ANTÓNIO, THE NATIVE-BORN PATRON SAINT OF LISBON, IS ONE HUGE CELEBRATION IN HIS HOMETOWN.

António was born during the high season for sardines and, eight hundred years after his birth, the Portuguese gulp loads of the little silver fish in his honor. There is also symbolism in the eating of sardines for António's birthday. It is said that when no one would listen to his sermons, the fish were the only ones that did. In sync, they all put their ears up in the air and, seeing this phenomenon, the Portuguese people began to recognize António's gift.

António was born on June 13th, which is today a holiday filled with festivities. The evening before, things start to really heat up. Every neighborhood in Lisbon has its own parade , each one more dazzling than the other. People build altars for the saint on the street and in their houses. Marching bands play in the streets and on open air stages, traditional fado music is sung, all under images of the birthday boy. Sardines can be bought by the dozen in the narrow streets and wine is served in plastic cups.

On the 13th itself, there is a special mass in the church of Santo António. Worshippers buy little bread rolls which they prick on the fence as a form of sacrifice. Next to the rolls they leave notes containing wishes they hope Saint António will fulfill. For poor couples in love, a wish will already come true that afternoon. Since António is also the patron saint of marriage, the city of Lisbon offers couples who are low on funds the opportunity to get married for free on his birthday. To celebrate their love, couples are driven in fancy cars around the city, alongside all the decorations of altars, garlands, and the empty cups that are still there from the revelry of the night before.

👍 **TIPS**

In the neighborhoods of Alfama and Mouraria, people continue partying till dawn.

🌐 **PORTUGAL**

Lisbon, Portugal.

🏵 **ORIGIN**

Santo António was born in 1195 in Lisbon; nevertheless, he's better known as Santo António de Padua, the city where he died. Through his wanderings, special deeds, and beautiful sermons, he became famous and loved. When he died, all church bells started ringing spontaneously. The house where he was born was already transformed into a religious site in the 15th century.

Bodypaint 48 Festival

THE MODELS ARE SUPPOSEDLY WEARING UNDERWEAR, BUT IT'S HIDDEN UNDER LAYERS OF PAINT. HARDLY ANYTHING OF THE BODY IS LEFT TO SEE. SHIELDS ON BREASTS, FLAMES ON BOTTOMS, YOU'LL SEE IT ALL AT THIS FESTIVAL IN AUSTRIA. THE CREATIVE GENIUSES EVEN ADD SOME FEATHERS, FUTURISTIC MASKS, AND OTHER EMBELLISH-MENTS.

And don't think the painters just haphazardly smear some colors on the bodies; everything has been carefully thought out. Every year has a theme, like Subcultures or the Renaissance, and the artists come to the festival with an exact plan. Entire stories are told, world views represented, and mythical legends depicted, all using the bodies as canvases.

The crème de la crème of the body painting world assembles each summer in Portschach, Austria, and spectators come from all over to admire the stunning creations. The audience can also get a glimpse of how the artists work. Inside the festival grounds, called Bodypaint City, the artists prep their models in open party tents. The patient models remain immobile for hours at a time, arms in the air if necessary, and let the brushes, sponges and airbrushing work their magic. Once they've undergone their transformations, the models parade through the City to be admired and then do a turn on the big stage. They also must pass by the judges, since, for the artists, this is the world championships. Points are awarded in all categories, particularly on the technical aspects. In the special effects category, the artist can dress up the body with whatever he fancies. This last category is the most spectacular: aliens, injured knights, futuristic green-eyed monsters, disfigured poison victims, fairytale princesses, fantasy elves and many more. It's incredible to imagine that a simple human body can be turned into something this beautiful and different.

All the bodies are pieces of art for merely one day. Perhaps that's why everyone, from visitors to seasoned professionals, goes crazy with their cameras. Because, just like street art, you are sure of one thing: it will disappear. The model will eventually take a shower with a huge bottle of soap, only to be transformed into another creature the following day.

For the audience there is more to this festival than just stands and walking artwork. There is live music, DJs, model shows, and fireworks. On one of the evenings, there is a black light performance. You guessed it: the tight, naked torsos are decorated with neon paint. But don't worry that the artists here take themselves too seriously; they also have a sense of humor. After all, this is not art with a capital A, but rather art that is not too highbrow to be accompanied by raucous beer drinking and all-night partying.

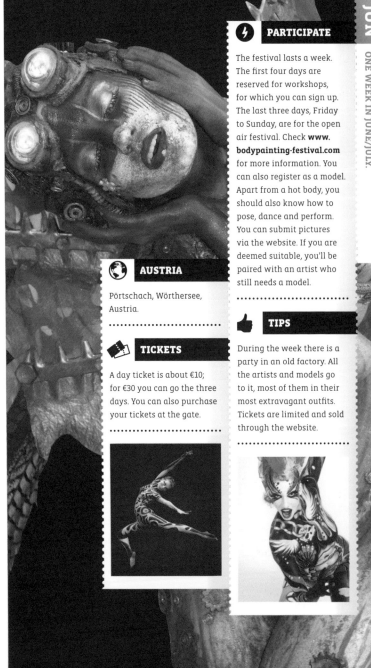

⚡ PARTICIPATE

The festival lasts a week. The first four days are reserved for workshops, for which you can sign up. The last three days, Friday to Sunday, are for the open air festival. Check **www.bodypainting-festival.com** for more information. You can also register as a model. Apart from a hot body, you should also know how to pose, dance and perform. You can submit pictures via the website. If you are deemed suitable, you'll be paired with an artist who still needs a model.

🌐 AUSTRIA

Pörtschach, Wörthersee, Austria.

🎟 TICKETS

A day ticket is about €10; for €30 you can go the three days. You can also purchase your tickets at the gate.

👍 TIPS

During the week there is a party in an old factory. All the artists and models go to it, most of them in their most extravagant outfits. Tickets are limited and sold through the website.

Naked Bike Ride

ACTIVISTS ARE NOT ALL BORING AND UGLY, ESPECIALLY WHEN THEY'RE AGITATING FOR A GOOD CAUSE. DURING THE ANNUAL NAKED BIKE RIDE, YOU'LL SEE MORE THAN YOUR FAIR SHARE OF NAKED BREASTS AND SWINGING DICKS PASSING BY IN A FLURRY OF TIRES AND SPOKES. THIS BIKE RIDE IS ALL ABOUT FULL EXPOSURE, IN BOTH THE PHYSICAL AND POLITICAL SENSES.

The old and fat take part alongside the young and muscular. The official mission of the bike ride is to reclaim the air from the car-driving, motorcycle-riding masses in a way that is "body-positive." Using naked bodies to achieve this goal is intended not only to provoke the public and the authorities and to garner media attention, but also to highlight the vulnerability of users of non-motorized forms of transport. Besides cyclists, the event welcomes skateboarders, as well as people in wheelchairs and other vehicles that need nothing but one's own body to be driven.

The first Naked Bike Ride was held in 2001 in Zaragoza, Spain. The original event is still one of the largest and most wild Naked Bike Rides, although some seventy towns and cities now host

their own every year. Sometimes the participants cover themselves in body paint or wear only a bikini, a bit of underwear or an outrageous costume. Because the organizers feel nobody should go naked who isn't fully comfortable with it, the dress code of the event is "Bare as you dare." Organizers warn the riders that there are hundreds of photographers and videographers camped out on the sidelines, and not just for respectable media outlets, but also for Flickr and dubious private collections. So there's a good chance that you and your painted breasts, bare buttocks and/or other private parts, might end up in a video on YouTube – way to get your political message out there!

49

 PARTICIPATE

Joining is free and can be spontaneous. If you don't have a bike, you can run naked. You can rent bikes or skates to participate, or use a folding bike, skateboard, or roller skates. For a list of countries where you can bare it all while biking for a good cause, visit **www.worldnakedbikeride.org**.

TIPS

How naked you can get while participating depends on the rules of the particular country; the local organization can provide you with these rules. For example, in Vermont it is legal to be naked on public roads, but not to undress in public. In Zaragoza and the rest of Spain, you are permitted to be naked in the street as long as you do not become obscene.

 SPAIN

The center of Zaragoza, Spain.

ANNO **ORIGIN**

The event was started by activists in 2001, for a variety of reasons: to reclaim the streets from motorized vehicle-driving multitudes; as an indictment of an oil-dependent society; as a protest against pollution, and more. And, of course, to have some fun and harass the authorities a little.

Calcio Storico

THE MACHO FLORENTINE MEN HAVE NO NEED FOR WOMEN IN ORDER TO SHOW OFF THEIR MANHOOD. THEY DO THIS INSTEAD BY BEATING EACH OTHER SENSELESS EVERY JUNE IN A GAME OF PRIMITIVE FOOTBALL CALLED CALCIO STORICO.

Calcio Storico, a sport with aristocratic origins that was even played by popes, dates back to 16th century Florence. It closely resembles a game of rugby, but without rules. Yet even without set rules, it is expected that players will exercise some measure of self-control while playing this noble sport. Played on a sand-covered square surrounded by short, strong walls, a game of Calcio Storico is an impressive show of pageantry and violence. One team of twenty-seven men, outfitted in brilliant, Renaissance-inspired costumes, plays against another team of twenty-seven men in equally eye-catching, but differently colored, attire. Four teams, each in the colors of their district of Florence, compete in the annual tournament.

The teams have 50 minutes to score as many goals as possible. They do this by getting the ball over the wooden wall at the other end of the field - by whatever means necessary. To score a goal, almost anything is permitted. While the game is overseen by six referees, a referee will only call a foul if a player kicks another player in the back or sucker punches him. Otherwise, the referees will simply wave their ostrich feather plumes in the enraged faces of the players and allow the game to continue.

In Calcio Storico, fights break out all over the field and players often tear their opponents costumes to shreds. As a rule of thumb, it's best for a player to somehow disable his opponent before that opponent gets too close to the goal. Since players cannot be substituted, any player who knocks out an opposing player, or breaks a few legs, is doing his team some good.

Men with criminal records are not allowed to play on any of the four teams. That is not necessarily to maintain safety on the field, but to try to minimize the possibility of serious clashes towards the end of the game.

For the spectators, Calcio Storico is an entertaining and chaotic spectacle. Because the four teams represent different districts in Florence, the Florentines watching the game get quite animated. The women in the crowd can become especially heated as the players' costumes get ripped off, revealing heavily muscled men running around only in glittered thongs.

50

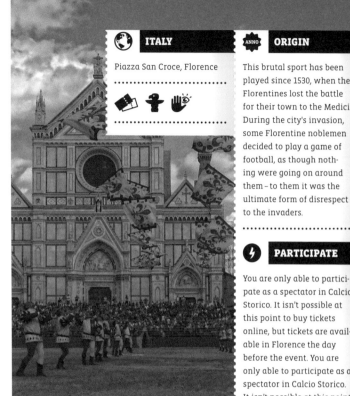

JUN

THE FINAL IS ON JUNE 24TH, THE SEMIFINALS ARE TWO SUNDAYS BEFORE THAT.

ITALY

Piazza San Croce, Florence

ORIGIN

This brutal sport has been played since 1530, when the Florentines lost the battle for their town to the Medici. During the city's invasion, some Florentine noblemen decided to play a game of football, as though nothing were going on around them – to them it was the ultimate form of disrespect to the invaders.

PARTICIPATE

You are only able to participate as a spectator in Calcio Storico. It isn't possible at this point to buy tickets online, but tickets are available in Florence the day before the event. You are only able to participate as a spectator in Calcio Storico. It isn't possible at this point to buy tickets online, but tickets are readily available in Florence the day before the event.

Stonehenge

LOOKING FOR A NEW WAY TO CELEBRATE THE SUMMER SOLSTICE THIS YEAR? COME TO STONEHENGE AND JOIN THE DRUIDS, WICCAN PRIESTESSES, NEO-HIPPIES, AND OTHER PEOPLE – LOOKING TO GET CLOSER TO NATURE – WHO GATHER HERE TO WATCH THE SUN TRAVEL TO ITS HIGHEST POINT IN THE SKY.

This ceremony, with pagan roots, occurs on the day in June when night is the shortest. Tens of thousands gather on the Salisbury Plain to celebrate the solstice at this special site. Some dress in rags to emphasize their natural state, others wear leaves and branches in their hair. There are drummers, jugglers, and lots of people dancing slowly in long skirts, arms outstretched. But ordinary citizens and those who hope to learn something about England's pagan history are also among the revelers.

Archaeologists still do not agree on exactly when Stonehenge was built. The prevailing theory is that work on this magnificent prehistoric monument spanned many centuries. In 3100 BC, the first holes were dug. A thousand years later, the giant stones – the heaviest weigh some forty-five tons – were dragged from hundreds of miles away to where they are today. There are those who say the stone circle is a cemetery, and others who believe it's a temple, a landing strip for aliens, an astrological calendar, or a place to worship the sun. Those last two theories arise because of the placement of the stones in relation to where the sun rises during the summer and winter solstices. During the summer solstice, sunlight hits slightly past the Heel Stone just outside the circle. Some

51

 ENGLAND

Stonehenge in southern England.

 TIPS

Only at the solstice can you approach the stones up close, since this is not permitted during the rest of the year and barricades make it impossible.

 ORIGIN

Starting in 1972, alternative people began gathering at Stonehenge for a summer festival called the Stonehenge Free Festival. It grew into a grand annual festival for hippies and new-agers. In 1985, police wanted to stop the festival and "The Battle of the Beanfield" ensued, with policeman hitting the hippies who had withdrawn into the bean field. The celebration was banned until 1999, when people again were allowed to return for the solstice.

claim that in the past four thousand years the sun has shifted and that, thousands of years ago, the solstice at Stonehenge looked much more spectacular. It is these theories that draw all the people to the solstice celebration, at which they believe something magical happens.

All night long they stay out there, beating their drums, shaking their tambourines. And when the sun almost rises, around a quarter to five in the morning, many begin stabbing their hands in the air in worship. Some meditate. It would be nice and dramatic if the warm sunlight would then wash over the worshippers' blissful faces, but this is England. The sun is usually obscured by a layer of clouds and the sky just brightens up a bit. At eight in the morning, everyone must pack up their bongo drums, vacate the grounds, and leave Stonehenge to the hordes of paying tourists.

52 San Joan

A PERSON FROM THE MIDDLE AGES TRANSPORTED TO THE FESTIVAL OF SAN JOAN IN MENORCA WOULD FEEL RIGHT AT HOME. HE COULD LIKELY APPRECIATE THE SIGHT OF ALL THE HORSES UP ON THEIR HIND LEGS, WALKING AROUND, A MAJOR ELEMENT OF THIS FIESTA.

Even more startling to see than those horses is what the locals call the *Homo des Be* – a man dressed in lambskins, crosses painted on his hands and bare feet, who carries a live lamb on his shoulders. The lamb is the living symbol of St. John the Baptist (Joan, in Catalan), and, on the Sunday prior to the feast day of San Joan, it is presented to the city. After this somber procession, the party begins in Ciutadella. And what better way to start a fiesta than with a hazelnut fight? How this bizarre tradition originated is not entirely clear, but it could be that centuries ago hazelnuts were used against witches. Some people also say that throwing sacks of hazelnuts at each other is a sign of love.

The spectacular show of the strong Menorcan horses takes place in the Plaza des Born. Ridden by horsemen in colorful medieval attire, each representing a social class, the black, muscular animals gallop around the crowded square. The horses rear back on their hind legs, front legs high in the air. Those legs come down dangerously close to the people on the ground, but the celebrants are not afraid, despite the fact there are no fences separating the spectators from the horses. Everyone wants to touch the horses. Each horse is surrounded by throngs of ardent admirers.

A day later, on the official birthday of San Joan, the townspeople engage in a reenactment, and there is drinking and dancing into the night. The drink of choice is called *pomada,* a powerful mix of Mahon gin and lemonade. The fireworks explode overhead when a particular song is played, indicating that this year's festivities are coming to an end. Until next year!

SPAIN

Ciutadella, Menorca, Spain.

TIPS

If you are even a little bit afraid of horses, don't stand in the square during the horse shows. The animals race through everything and everyone.

ORIGIN

The night before San Joan, June 23, is the shortest night of the year in the northern hemisphere. This endless night has been celebrated since pre-Christian times as the victory of light over darkness. San Joan is celebrated throughout Spain, but since Menorca, one of the Balearic Islands, is quite remote, its festivities, costumes, and flags, have remained unchanged for centuries and are a mixture of pagan and Catholic rituals and symbols.

Inti Raymi

53

FIVE HUNDRED ACTORS DRESSED IN FULL INCA REGALIA HIKE THROUGH THE FLOWER-ADORNED STREETS OF CUZCO TOWARD THE OLD INCA FORTRESS ABOVE THE CITY TO MAKE A SACRIFICE TO THE SUN AND MOTHER NATURE. THOUSANDS CHEER THEM AS THEY MARCH, AND THOUSANDS MORE GREET THEM WHEN THEY REACH THE FORTRESS.

The white, fluffy llama is no longer sacrificed for real, its heart is not pulled out of its body while still beating and its intestines are no longer used to predict the future. Nonetheless, the actors make it all seem very real and serious. The events begin in the morning. The procession starts in Cuzco, near the Santo Domingo church, which the Catholics cleverly built over the Incan Temple of the Sun. The procession of extras is led by an actor playing an Inca chief, Sapa Inca, who is carried in a golden carriage. Accompanied by singing, praying, and dancing, the procession passes by Plaza des Armas – an important place for the Incas before the Spanish conquest - to Sachsayhuamán (tourists are allowed to pronounce this as 'sexy woman'), a sacred ancient fortress. There the celebration continues with dances, the llama "sacrifice," and a speech in Quechua, the Inca language that is still spoken by natives.

⚡ **PARTICIPATE**

Watching everything in Cuzco is free, but to witness the rituals on Sachsayhuamán, you will need to buy a ticket. These can be quite pricey, about $90, and are for sale on **www.emufec.gob.pe**. If you prefer to go the free ride route, be sure to make it early in the morning to Plaza des Armas, or make a reservation for a table with a nice view in one of the restaurants that overlook the plaza. When the sun sets, the street party begins in Cuzco (where in fact, every night is a party). You will still see a lot of people in Inca costumes, local attire and Mardi Gras-style outfits.

🏛 **ORIGIN**

During the Inca times, Inti Raymi was the most important ceremony of the year. The last time Inti Raymi was celebrated in the presence of an Inca emperor was in 1535. In 1944, some descendants of the native people of Peru performed a historical reconstruction of Inti Raymi for the first time.

🌐 **PERU**

Cuzco and the nearby site of Sachsayhuamán.

Although the Inti Raymi performance may be a spectacle for tourists, it is also done for and by the descendants of the Incas, who proudly celebrate their heritage. Inti Raymi takes place on the winter solstice, June 24, just as it did before the Spaniards prohibited it in 1572. The indigenous people still celebrate this day as a moment to request a good harvest from the gods and to thank them for the year that has passed. Not just in and around Cuzco, but everywhere where descendants of the Incas live, they raise their glasses. In the streets and around the plaza of Cuzco, there is a big party on the evening of Inti Raymi, complete with bands, chicha, beer, and, of course, pisco sours, the famous peruvian drink.

PERU

CUZCO

Kirkpınar

WHILE THE AVERAGE WOMAN MIGHT KNOW THE NAMES OF A FEW HOT STAR ATHLETICS, IT'S PRETTY DOUBTFUL SHE CAN NAME TOO MANY OIL WRESTLERS. AND THAT'S A SHAME, SINCE THE WORLD CHAMPIONSHIPS OF TURKEY'S NATIONAL SPORT IS A PARADISE FOR THE LADIES (AND ANYONE ELSE WHO APPRECIATES THE SIGHT OF WELL-OILED, MUSCULAR, HALF-NAKED MEN COMPETING IN AN ANCIENT SPORT).

The locals of Edirne, the town where this wrestling extravaganza is held, were shocked when a Turkish gay organization offered bus tours to Kırkpınar. But perhaps it should not have come as a surprise at all, given the talent on display. Off the field, the tournament itself offers little in the way of glamour or sophistication, but it does have its good points. Natural tea delights abound. And a cold Efes beer tastes just fine, even when sitting on an old plastic lawn chair.

The competition lasts for three days and spans multiple categories, from the school boys to the over-40 veterans. Under a baking sun, about 1,000 elite wrestlers compete. They are barefoot, stripped to the waist, and wearing only the traditional oiled leather pants. The style of fighting might best be described as "anything goes" – there are few rules and matches have no time limits. Only if a match goes over a half-hour will it be decided by sudden death. And, unlike in other forms of wrestling, there are few forbidden holds and it's not against the rules to grab an opponent's pants, slippery as they may be.

There are wrestling competitions held throughout Turkey, but Kırkpınar is the oldest (since 1362) and most prestigious. All the top wrestlers attend, and wealthy businessmen eagerly sponsor the contenders. On the third day, when the finals take place, the President of Turkey comes to Edirne to congratulate the winners. And if the *bass pehlival* (head wrestler) wins the gold belt prize three consecutive times, he may keep it.

54

TURKEY

On a field near Edirne, Turkey (near the border with Bulgaria).

👍 TIPS

The huge, heavily-muscled grapplers are naturally the most important and thus attract the most public attention. But keep an eye on the young ones: they're slender, agile and lightning fast, and thus might be more fun to watch (unless you're into really wide torsos).

⚡ ORIGIN

The men in the region have been oil wrestling for centuries. It is suspected that oil came into play because the area was plagued with malaria-carrying mosquitoes. One of the remedies to protect oneself from mosquitoes was to put on a lot of olive oil. Even when the oil was not longer needed for protective purposes, it remained a part of the sport. Indeed, people found that wrestling with oil was more fun. Kırkpınar has been taking place since 1362, and during all these centuries, it's only been canceled seventy times. However, the tournament has changed location a few times.

Gettysburg Civil War Reenactment

YOU WON'T SET ONE FOOT ON THE BATTLEFIELD AT GETTYS-
BURG WITH SNEAKERS UNDER YOUR NINETEENTH-CENTURY
MILITARY UNIFORM. ALTHOUGH THE AUDIENCE MAY BE AT A
CONSIDERABLE DISTANCE FROM THE CANNONS, THE BATTLE
IS NEVERTHELESS RECREATED ACCURATELY, DOWN TO THE
SMALLEST DETAILS.

The men on the battlefield have been practicing for months to be able to
reenact the bloodiest battle of the American Civil War. Around fifty thousand
soldiers died during the three day battle at Gettysburg in 1863, and what
began as an event commemorating those who fell has become a spectacle
for tourists and history buffs attracting hordes of visitors every year.
There are reenactments of Civil War battles throughout the United States,
but the one at Gettysburg is the biggest. Tens of thousands of people are
drawn to it – both to participate and to watch. But it's not possible to just

55

UNITED STATES

Gettysburg, Pennsylvania, United States.

....

 TICKETS

Tickets for three days cost about $30.

....

 PARTICIPATE

You cannot just hop in. Participation is only for the diehards who have been members of one of the hundreds of American reenactment teams. You could, however, sign up to walk around at the side programs in your authentic outfit (and with authentic behavior). Check **www.gettysburggreenactment.com** for details.

....

DICTIONARY

⚡ **Farb:** Reenactor who puts little time and money into rendering his outfit and performance authentic. It is the farb who will be out on the field lighting a modern filtered cigarette. They are also called *polyester soldiers*.

⚡ **Stitch nazi:** Opposite of a farb. The reenactor who wants to execute every detail absolutely perfectly, all the way down to the stitches that were used to make the clothing.

⚡ **Take a hit:** Pretend to die.

....

ORIGIN

Battles of the American Civil War were already being recreated before the conflict was even over. Veterans reenacted parts of the battle to honor their fallen comrades and to demonstrate to others what had happened. Fifty years after the Battle of Gettysburg, the Great Reunion was held in 1913, to which fifty thousand veterans showed up on both the Union and Confederate sides. At the Reunion, the battle was reenacted. Reenactment as a hobby appears to have really begun to flourish in the 1960s, a hundred years after the Battle of Gettysburg, when there was a lot of media attention around the battle and its specifics.

....

show up and join in the battle; you have to be a member of a reenactment group that has at least already 'fought' in a couple of smaller events. That is the only way for the organization to ensure that your shoes, uniform and artillery will be authentic. They don't want to see a musket being loaded by someone with a visible Casio watch on his wrist.

The battle is recreated as precisely as possible and the entire event transpires within a strict time table. Each division knows in advance what its part is, to ensure that the battle progresses smoothly, while a narrator describes the bloody happenings on the battlefield. In addition to the highlights of the skirmishes, you can absorb a lot more about the war life and the Civil War period during this three day event. There are talks about the life of a soldier during the Civil War, and displays of war weddings. You can also attend an emergency surgery procedure in the civil war hospital, overhear strategic discussions between top officers, and so on. Here and there, spread out on the nearby fields, you'll see people sitting in tents, dressed as in the old days. These hobbyists embroider, play the guitar or read a book. The modern American woman who wants to participate in the reenactment has to do it here, since she cannot set a foot on the battlefield, because women did not take part in the fighting. After all, it all has to be authentic. SUVs, as well, are left behind in the reenactors' parking lot.

Il Palio

56

THE GALLOPING MADNESS AROUND SIENA'S PIAZZA DEL CAMPO TAKES JUST NINETY SECONDS. BUT WHAT AN EXHILARATING MINUTE AND A HALF IT IS.

The build up to the race, called Il Palio, full of elaborate, centuries-old rituals and pageantry. Four days prior to the event, the race course is prepared and the ground of the Campo covered with mud. Any potentially dangerous angle is padded with crash barriers – in case a horse, in the frenzy of it all, throws his jockey towards a wall or the grandstands. On the day in which the horses for the different *contrade* are selected, the Sienese and tourists alike walk by to discuss the condition of the horses, debate the merits of the numerous jockeys, and, of course, place some bets.

Each jockey represents one of the seventeen contrade, or districts, of Siena, and each contrada has its own colors, flag, and symbol. Like an eagle, a snail, a shell, and a she-wolf. The residents of the different contrade are fiercely proud of their districts and wave their district flags with great passion. Of the seventeen, only ten contrade are allowed to participate in the race. Which ones will get to take part in any given year is partly determined by an ancient set of rules and partly by a lottery.

After the horses have been selected, both horse and jockey are blessed by the church of the district that they will be representing. While that is happening, the magnificent and colorful parade of splendidly-dressed Sienese in medieval costumes winds through town towards the Campo. An unforgettable flag throwing display is also a treasured element of the pre-race pageantry. Once the parade reaches the Campo and the horses are about to enter, the crowd is nearly delirious with excitement and anticipation.

The arena could not be more packed - thirty thousand people sit in the grandstands, while tens of thousands fortunate spectators try to find themselves spots on the narrow terraces, roofs, balconies, ladders, or even the scaffolding around the square. The horses run three laps around the square, the jockeys riding bareback, and pretty much anything is permitted. Jockeys whip not only their own horses, but also the other horses and their riders, and there is lots of pushing and shoving. Spurred on by the cheers of the crowd, a jockey will do anything to finish first and win the coveted *pallium*, the silk banner after which the race is named, for his contrada.

The end of the race obviously means glory, and much flag-waving, for the residents of one lucky contrada, but it also heralds the beginning of an enormous party for everyone. After all, there are ultimately more winners than losers at the Palio.

ITALY

Piazza del Campo,
Siena, Italy.

ORIGIN

In the 17th century, the
Virgin Mary is said to have
appeared in Siena, and to
celebrate this miraculous
event, the first Palio was
held on August 16, 1656.

TIPS

⚡ The spots in the middle of
the Campo, which are sur-
rounded by the race track,
are free and open to eve-
ryone. Make sure you get
there at least four hours
early should you hope
to secure one of these
places. The gates close at
half past four, at which
point the preparations
for the procession around
the square begin, and the
gates are reopened after
the race. Those who suffer
from claustrophobia or
agoraphobia, or a mixture
of both, might be better
off not attending. If you
will be sitting or standing
in the Campo, make sure
to bring enough food and
water. It can be hot and
there are no vendors selling refreshments.

⚡ You can also check out
more about the race and
the festivities at
www.ilpalio.org.

Ufo Festival

ALL THE FREAKS COME OUT, IN THEIR GREEN ALIEN SUITS COMPLETE WITH ANTENNAE. FOR THREE DAYS, THE STREETS OF ROSWELL, NEW MEXICO ARE CRAWLING WITH THOUSANDS OF EXTRA-TERRESTRIALS HAVING THE TIME OF THEIR LIVES.

The parade on Saturday is the highlight of the festival. This event attracts twenty thousand people, including those who want to flaunt their alienness and those who want to gawk at the people who believe they have a connection with aliens. There are classic green Martians present, of course, but also modern interpretations of extraterrestrial life such as blue Avatars. Needless to say, there are all manner of crazy-looking outfits: more feelers and antennae than you could imagine, and many costumes featuring disproportionately large or small heads. And you'll be relieved to learn that pets are not left out of the festivities in Roswell. In the week preceding the parade, there is a special contest for Alien Pets.

For these three days, the Roswell UFO Festival offers a haven for all those who firmly believe that aliens exist. They can have their suspicions confirmed at different lectures and can discuss their own abduction experiences during workshops. For non-believing earthlings, the festival offers an entertaining glimpse into alien obsession and an excuse to dress up.

A visit to the International UFO Museum and Research Center, is mandatory. Of course everyone who attends the festival is more than familiar with the Roswell incident of 1947. Was it a flying saucer that crashed, leaving eleven dead alien bodies, or was it a high-tech blimp performing surveillance on the Russians? Whatever it was, it made Roswell famous. Even when the festival is not taking place, the town still celebrates the extraordinary event – even the local McDonald's is housed in a flying saucer.

57

UNITED STATES

Roswell, New Mexico, USA.

PARTICIPATE

Put on your E.T. suit and join the parade. But please note that in July it's blazing hot in New Mexico and that latex is not the most breathable fabric. Make sure to sign up for the best-dressed competition and the flying saucer throwing in advance. Find out more at **www.ufofestivalroswell.com**.

ORIGIN

The incident happened in 1947. That's when the mysterious discovery was made. The festival has been organized since 1998, to bring some life and extra revenue to this small, somewhat nondescript town.

Bous a la Mar

BOUS A LA MAR OFFERS BULL RUNNING FOR BEGINNERS. IF THE RUNNING BULL, DROOLING WITH ANGER, IS DETERMINED TO PIERCE YOU WITH HIS HORNS, THEN YOU'VE GOT A SIMPLE ESCAPE ROUTE: JUMPING INTO THE MEDITERRANEAN SEA. THE BULL WILL SOMETIMES CHASE YOU INTO THE SEA, BUT IN THE WAVES HE CAN DO NOTHING.

If you love animals, rest assured that the bulls do not drown. A couple of boats stand ready to lasso them and tow them back to shore. Not long after his dip in the sea, the bull is ready for his next run. Bous a la Mar is the culmination of a week-long celebration in Denia, a beautiful old town in southeastern Spain, near the city of Alicante. On the Sunday of the festival, everyone gathers in the streets of Denia to drink and dance to live music. Many friends and family groups wear specially printed T-shirts bearing funny slogans or just their names. But there is also an air of anxiety in the air during the festivities since everyone knows that the bulls will be arriving shortly. And no one wants to be the one still drinking and gossiping in the street when the bulls come through.

The bulls run down the main street of town and eventually arrive in a ring on the quay. The stadium has three sides for the stands with the fourth left open to the sea. Once the bulls arrive in the ring, dozens of young men challenge and irritate the bulls in an effort to get the bulls angry enough to pursue them into the sea. When the bulls chase after the young men into the sea, the audience erupts in applause.

58

ON A SUNDAY DURING LAS
FIESTAS DE LA SANTÍSIMA
SANGRE, IN JULY.

🌐 **SPAIN**

Denia, Spain.

🏅 **ORIGIN**

The running of the bulls is a
Spanish phenomenon that
has been happening for
centuries, most famously in
Pamplona. Bous a la Mar has
been held since 1925.

👍 **TIPS**

For the full festival and the
times of the bull run visit
www.denia.net.

⚡ **PARTICIPATE**

Feel free to participate if
you've got the *cojones*. You
can even join in if you're
already sitting in the stands
and decide that you want
to be a part of the action.
Anyone sober and capable
of running can enter the
arena.

Eukonkanto

IT'S SO INCREDIBLY EROTIC, THROWING A WOMAN OVER YOUR SHOULDER AND HOBBLING THROUGH AN OBSTACLE COURSE. AND YOU, TOO, CAN DO THIS DURING THE FINNISH EUKONKANTO, OR WOMAN CARRYING RACE. RHYTHM, HARMONY, INTIMACY, TOUCHING EACH OTHER'S BODIES...

The women are carried 253.5 meters (around 760 feet) and are shaken so much that a helmet is mandatory. You might think that the women would want to dress in a fashionable manner for this event, but those who take this seriously know to wear only a sports bra and biking shorts. When the woman is hanging upside down against her partner's back with her legs clamped around his neck, this is also a tactical must.

Every carrying technique is permitted: thrown over the shoulder, straddling the back, or held in the arms. But whoever drops his precious cargo - even one foot on the ground counts- receives penalty time. And that's no good, since the couple that crosses the line first wins. Arguing the penalty time is not just an option, it's actually written into the extended rules. However, this must be done in writing within 15 minutes after finishing the race at a cost of € 50.

The spirit of the competition lies somewhere between the incredibly funny and the deadly serious . As if perfectly rehearsed, fanatics can be seen ferrying their skinny women skillfully through the water obstacles, then dunking the women in the water, then following that feat by deftly jumping two hurdles. Others facing the same obstacle would take ten seconds to carefully place one leg, then the other, over the hurdle, but these trained athletes hop over the hurdles as if they were mere curbs on the street. The woman being carried doesn't necessarily have to be the partner of the person carrying her; there are also pairs that enter the event strictly for sporting purposes. Occasionally, someone brave even attempts it with a very heavy woman. There is an advantage to this: the winner receives the woman's weight in beer. Although there is no upper weight limit, the women cannot weigh less than 49 kilos (108 pounds). The leaner types must carry a backpack along to account for the missing weight. The public gets to see thousands of pairs racing against each other, most of them finishing the race in three minutes. The really fast couples that finish the race in a minute nervously watch the rest of the participants, hoping the later couples don't beat their time. The spectators are less serious while the event is under way. Finns love to drink, so the competitive day turns into a crazy night.

FINLAND

Sonkajärvi, Finland

PARTICIPATE

Talking part in the main race costs €50 per pair. Participating in the sprint is €20, while the race team event (three men pass off the woman like a baton) is €111 per team. You can register now at **www.eukonkanto.fi.** Practicing beforehand is recommended. Buying tickets to watch is possible, but at €20 a piece you might as well join in on the fun. For the less athletically-inclined pairs, there is a prize for best costume.

ORIGIN

The woman-carrying ritual appears to be a centuries old Finnish tradition. There are many (obviously) different versions about its origins. It could be a form of courtship: boys from one village would go to another village and would throw a girl over their shoulders to take back home with them. But the most appealing story may be that of the notorious 19th century bandit Herkko Rosvo-Ronkainen. He would test potential new gang members by making them run through a similar obstacle course. In addition, not only would he steal men's valuables, but he would also toss their wives over his shoulders and disappear into the dark forest. Eukonkanto has been held since 1992.

60 Running of the Bulls

ANXIETY CAN STRIKE MOMENTS BEFORE THE RACE BEGINS, BUT THERE IS NO TURNING BACK. THIS IS THE ANNUAL RUNNING OF THE BULLS IN PAMPLONA.

Since 1910, there have been fifteen deaths, mostly locals, as well as thousands of injuries. Not all of those were killed by the bulls, but sometimes by other ailments. Yet, despite the dangers, thousands of people still participate every year in these eight days of bull running. The Spaniards call the event the *encierro*, from the verb meaning "to lock up" or "to pen." The purpose of the race is for the bulls to travel from the corrals where they have spent the previous evening to the bullring, where they will be killed later in the day. The encierro itself is likely a bigger attraction than the bullfight.

As early as 4 a.m., the first spectators start lining up. Starting at 8 a.m., the runners, their adrenaline pumping, hear the sound of a rocket that denotes the release of the bulls from their corrals.

A few minutes later, the madness begins as the runners and the bulls pass by, in a blink (the whole event normally lasts only three or four minutes). Then, once all the bulls have entered the stadium, people assess the damage and help out any of the runners or spectators who have been injured. After that, the spectators make their way to the bars of Pamplona – even though it is still early morning – to bask in the reflected glory of the runners. Or perhaps to celebrate their relief at not having been injured.

In Pamplona, this is all part of the famous festival of San Fermín, the patron saint of Pamplona, who was beheaded in the year 303. Hence the red scarf you will need to tie around your neck if you really want to be like the locals.

JUL

ANNUALLY, STARTING AT 12 NOON ON JULY 6 TO MIDNIGHT ON JULY 14.

SPAIN

Pamplona, Spain.

TIPS

⚡ The race is about to begin when the runners say a prayer to San Fermín: 'A San Fermín pedimos, por ser nuestro patrón, nos en el encierro guíe dándonos subendicion.'

⚡ If you fall, try not to stand up. Curl yourself into a ball, face down, arms around your head. Stand up only when the spectators tell you it is safe.

LEGEND

1 Corralillos
2 Cuesta de Santa Domingo
3 Plaza del Ayuntamiento
4 Curva de Mercaderes hacia Estafeta
5 Calle Estafeta
6 Curva de Telefónica
7 Callejón
8 Plaza de Toros
9 Plaza del Castillo

ORIGIN

Spaniards have been running with the bulls since the 14th century. It began when farmers would chase their bulls to get them to the market faster. Boys started to run with the bulls to show their toughness, and this became a popular ritual – not only in Pamplona, but also in many places in Spain and Portugal.

PARTICIPATE

⚡ **As a runner:**
If you want to sprint with a roaring bull behind you and run the risk of being furiously thrown against the wall by 650 pounds of muscle, then the place to do this is in Pamplona. Any sober, fit adult in white pants, a white shirt, and a red scarf can participate. Show up no later than 6:30 a.m. at the small square at the beginning of the route.

⚡ **As a spectator:**
For a spot with a good view, you'll need to stand along the course beginning around 4 or 5 a.m. You can book a place in a hotel or hostel at least nine months in advance, and that is recommended. And keep in mind that the spectators dress in the same outfits as the runners.

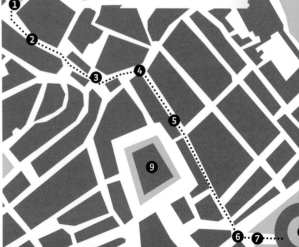

Amtrak Mooning

IN THE BEGINNING, IT SEEMS LIKE A HUGE SWINGERS GATHERING. THOUSANDS OF WOMEN HANGING FROM THEIR CAMPERS, SQUEEZING THEIR BREASTS, AND TRYING TO EARN A FREE TEQUILA SHOT OR A CHEAP NECKLACE. SOMETIMES, JUST FOR THE FUN OF IT, THE 'LADIES' LIFT THEIR SKIRTS AND SHOW THEIR (MORE OFTEN THAN NOT UNSHAVED) AREA BELOW. AT LEAST THAT WAS THE CASE UNTIL 2008, WHEN POLICE FINALLY INTERVENED AND INTRODUCED A NEW SET OF RULES FOR THE CLOTHING-CHALLENGED INDIVIDUALS. SINCE THEN, NO MORE EXPOSED GENITALIA OR ALCOHOL HAVE BEEN ALLOWED ON THE PUBLIC ROADS.

Since the changes of 2008, this has evolved into a tradition of people flashing their bare butts to the passing Amtrak passengers. Although it seems innocent enough, you can imagine some very white bare assets reflecting the sun and blinding a few unlucky passersby. Even at night, the participants kindly shine a flashlight on themselves to be sure the passengers on the trains get a great view and don't miss a thing. The location for the before- and after-partying, since the new rules went into effect, is the Mugs Away Saloon. Customers enjoying their favorite alcoholic beverage rush outside as soon as they hear a train coming to show off their talents – pants down and ass out against the fence. Then everyone heads back to their drinks to await the next train.

Until 2006, there weren't many trains that came through the Laguna Niguel route; but now, with the addition of the local Metrolink line, there is even more exposure available. To please both the passengers and those who are doing the mooning, the trains have a tendency to slow down a bit while passing through the mooning area, although passengers still need to watch their videos in slow motion to get a good view of the action. So, participants aim to have their pants around their ankles and be ready against the fence when the train passes; something incredibly liberating in a puritan America. It's understandable that children are encouraged not to attend.

61

UNITED STATES

Mugs Away Saloon, 27324 Camino Capistrano, Laguna Niguel, California, USA.

TIPS

⚡ Take enough money with you to buy your own drinks, since the free rounds from KT Smith are nowhere to be found. Since the police intervention in 2008, the number of participants has dropped dramatically and parking has become quite difficult. But still try to arrive early in the day as the festival can often get quite crowded.

⚡ The sun is hot and bright so don't forget to protect your sensitive skin, especially if you plan to bare your butt!

ORIGIN

It began in 1979, when old KT Smith yelled, "A beer to anyone who goes outside and moons the train". Bar patrons immediately flew out the door to drop their drawers for the passing train, and the ecstatic drinking binge that followed had to be, of course, repeated the following year.

PARTICIPATE

Anyone who isn't afraid to bare all (your butt, that is) can participate. If you prefer to go the more prudish route, park your car at one of the nearby train stations and be sure to buy a return ticket.

62

Boryeong Mud Festival

 SOUTH KOREA **TIPS** **ORIGIN**

Daecheon Beach, Boryeong, South Korea.

Since 1998

TIPS

- There are long lines for showering the mineral-rich mud of your body. You can opt to take a plunge in the ocean to cleanse it off, if you can put up with the salt on your skin for the rest of the night.
- Check out all the details at **www.mudfestival. or.kr/english**.
- Don't leave your valuables lying around next to the wresting arena. Make sure to put them away in one of the lockers on the beach.

ORIGIN

The little town of Boryeong in South Korea found its identity when it was scientifically proven in 1996 that the mud from the surroundings were extremely beneficial. The mud was sold to the cosmetic industry, but the tourist agency thought they could get something extra out of the discovery, as well. The local mud festival has turned into one of the biggest events in South Korea. Over a million people come to the beach during these nine days.

A TROPICAL PARADISE FOR MUD LOVERS. SLIDES, SWIMMING POOLS, HOT TUBS, BARS, PARTIES AND WRESTLING CONTESTS; FOR NINE DAYS EVERY YEAR THE SMALL SOUTH KOREAN TOWN OF BORYEONG IS CRAMMED WITH ROWDY MUD ENTHUSIASTS.

There is also a cultural program with singing and dancing and some theater, but this festival is really all about Daecheon, the beautiful 3.5 kilometer-long beach near Boryeong. That's where you'll find more slides than you can imagine, as well as a self-massage bath that holds a dozen people. Daecheon is also home to the most bizarre creation of the festival organizers: the mud prison. In this prison, you can lock yourself up to be assaulted with mud by the other visitors. Even this, according to the festival's marketers, can be a romantic experience – you can lock yourself up in the mud prison with the one you love.

This festival has no roots dating back hundreds of years; rather, it was brought to life in the 1990s to promote the city and its mineral-rich mud. With great pride, the festival organizers tout the fact that, in 1996, it was scientifically proven that the mud near Boryeong is healthy, healing, and very good for the skin. Since that discovery, the mud has been incorporated into all kinds of cosmetics. And, since 1998, the famous natural resource of Boryeong has also been used to attract legions of tourists to this beach town to fool around in the beneficial mud.

As a side program to the main mud madness there are cosmetic workshops, and you can get mud massages and treatments. You can also make pottery with the special mud and can get your body painted with colored mud. For a dose of culture, you can take a shuttle bus (after you shower, of course) to one of the tourist attractions in the area, like one of the many temples. That way you can head into the evening's parties with some extra cultural knowledge to share with your new friends. And these are quite good parties since there is just as much alcohol flowing as mud.

Mwaka Kogwa

63

ADMIT IT: SOMETIMES YOU WOULD PREFER TO GIVE AN ANNOYING PERSON A TASTE OF YOUR FIST RATHER THAN ACT IN A CIVILIZED WAY. DURING MWAKA KOGWA IN ZANZIBAR, MEN FREELY BASH EACH OTHER WITH STICKS FOR A COUPLE OF HOURS, AND AFTERWARDS THEY PARTY THEIR WAY INTO THE NEW YEAR FREE OF ANY GRUDGES.

In addition to the thrashing with sticks, this melee can include running, sudden pushing, pulling, and attacks from behind. But this is a riot without rage that you can witness at ease. The hard batons of the old days have been replaced by softer branches of sugar cane and dried strips of banana tree. The ritual's purpose is to vent any hard feelings before the start of the new year. Two sets of brothers from opposite sides of the village instigate the open air fight and, shortly thereafter, the rest of the men in the village join the brawl. It can be harsh and aggressive, but it never goes too far.

The women watch the men fighting and sing about love and life. The lyrics to their songs are filled with messages for the men. For instance, "The man who refuses to buy me a new *khanga* (garment), will not make love to me". In the old days, this made the men beat even harder to vent their frustrations with the women. These days, the men respond to the ladies' provocations with their own witty retorts.

Mwaga Kogwa is only celebrated in Zanzibar, and the most exuberant observance is in Makunduchi in the southeast. The entire festival lasts four days, but the first day is the wildest because of the fights and other symbolic rituals. A reed hut that looks like a wigwam is set on fire, with people packed around it. The smoke from the fire is to predict the future. Women dance and chant around the burning hut while others throw rocks and dirt onto the fire to extinguish the flames. This act is carried out to make sure no one will die in a burning house the following year.

Once the frustrations have been worked out and the crucial rituals performed, it's time to celebrate the new year. There are piles of food to feast on, and tourists are invited to share in the indulgence. Later the party moves to the beach, where everyone dances until the new year begins.

TANZANIA

Makunduchi, Zanzibar, Tanzania.

👍 TIPS

The main part of Makunduchi is Muslim, so make sure to dress appropriately.

⚡ PARTICIPATE

Ripping a branch out of a tree and starting to beat the people around you is not going to win you any friends. The fight is only for the locals. What the locals would appreciate, however, is for you to join them for the feasting and the drinking, and especially the dancing.

ANNO ORIGIN

Mwaka Kogwa was once Noroez, the new year's celebration of the Persian calendar. Around the year 1000, the first Persians came to live in Zanzibar, and in the following centuries the Persian traditions have blended with those of the local population.

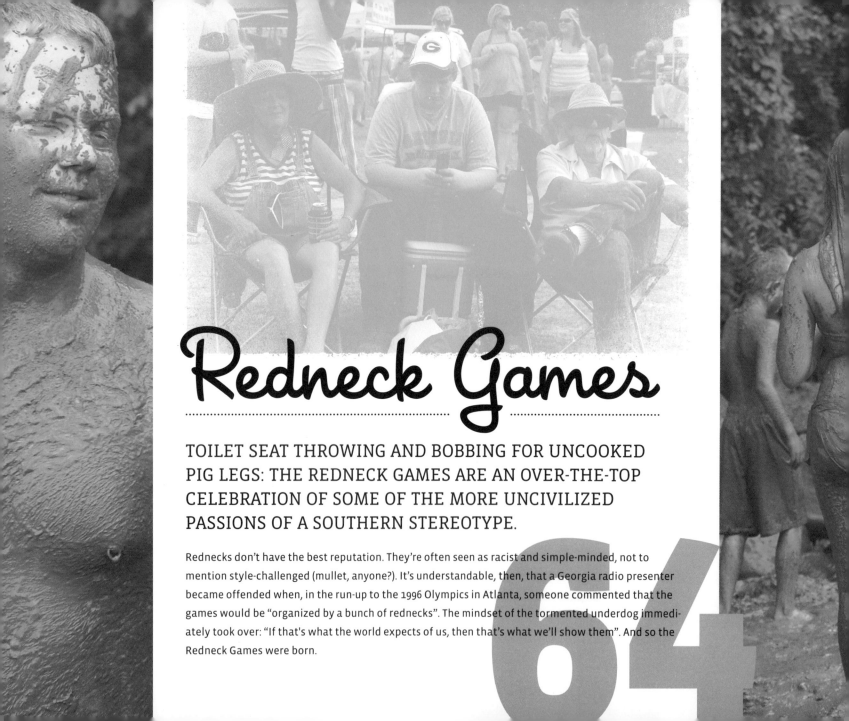

Redneck Games

TOILET SEAT THROWING AND BOBBING FOR UNCOOKED
PIG LEGS: THE REDNECK GAMES ARE AN OVER-THE-TOP
CELEBRATION OF SOME OF THE MORE UNCIVILIZED
PASSIONS OF A SOUTHERN STEREOTYPE.

Rednecks don't have the best reputation. They're often seen as racist and simple-minded, not to mention style-challenged (mullet, anyone?). It's understandable, then, that a Georgia radio presenter became offended when, in the run-up to the 1996 Olympics in Atlanta, someone commented that the games would be "organized by a bunch of rednecks". The mindset of the tormented underdog immediately took over: "If that's what the world expects of us, then that's what we'll show them". And so the Redneck Games were born.

64

UNITED STATES

East Dublin, Georgia, USA.

TIPS

Tickets cost five dollars a person. You can bring in a cooler, but no glass. For more information see **summerredneckgames.com**. Don't want to go alone? Go in advance to **www.redneckandsingle.com** to arrange a date.

PARTICIPATE

Put on your lumberjack shirt, pull down your jeans to make sure your crack is showing, and join the crowd. You can enter some "events" on the spot and you can always jump in the mud. Also try to practice a really good bad southern accent.

The "organizers" of these Games have stopped at nothing in an effort to reinforce every negative stereotype that exists about rednecks. Instead of a 50 meter swimming pool, there's a mud pit. Instead of an Olympic torch, there's a stick topped with a beer can that emits flames. There are contests involving toilet seat throwing, seed spitting, flipping cigarettes, and, naturally, wet t-shirts. There is also the truly unforgettable Armpit Serenade, in which contestants vie to create the most melodic and rhythmic noises possible from their own armpits. And, finally, the event that no one wants to miss: the mud pit belly flop. The higher the wet red earth splashes, the better. Last, but certainly not least, there's lots and lots of beer drinkin' to the sweet sounds of country music.

Rednecks according to Urban Dictionary
You would be a Redneck if:
• You have flowers planted in a bathroom appliance in your front yard
• Your wife weighs more than your refrigerator
• You can spit without opening your mouth

EAST DUBLIN

UNITED STATES

At Chabysh

65

EVEN A TWO-YEAR-OLD CAN RIDE A HORSE IN KYRGYZSTAN. RIDING HORSES IS LIKE BREATHING TO THE RURAL PEOPLE OF THIS CENTRAL ASIAN NATION, SO PERHAPS IT'S LOGICAL THAT THE LOCAL VARIATION OF SOCCER IS PLAYED ON HORSEBACK, WITH A DEAD GOAT AS THE BALL.

All the equestrian traditions of this nation come together during the celebration called At Chabysh, but the festival was actually created by foreigners worried about threats to the local horse breed. The communist Russians began to cross-breed the Kyrgyz horse with bigger racehorses from Western-Europe without thinking about the potential consequences.

Thanks to At Chabysh - because a breeding program was set up at the time of the first festival - the local horse breed has drawn the attention of the government again. The festival has also piqued the interest of adventurous tourists and generates some much-needed cash for the residents of a poor country in which two-thirds of the people live off the land.

At Chabysh is a kind of travelling festival that is organized a few times per year in different locations in Kyrgyzstan. The celebration of horse culture is the main element. The long-distance races featuring Kyrgyz horses are the highlight, as these horses are known for their stamina in the thin mountain air. The races are not necessarily about which horse crosses the 12, 15 or 35-kilometer finish line first, but about which horse is still the fittest after that kind of distance. Ultimately it's the veterinarians who determine which horse wins, after checking the temperature, heartbeat, and other vital functions of each horse.

The entertaining shows and games that take place during the festival are a daily pleasure for the population. One of these is rugby played with a goat corpse. In spring, shepherds still venture out by horse among the green pastures and pitch their yurts where they can. They occasionally slaughter a goat to eat. So, if you've got a dead goat in your midst, why not play a game of *Ulak Tartysh?* It is all about keeping the dead goat in your possession. Before one of the players is able to finally take off with the loot, the game looks like a big free-for-all, not unlike a little kids' soccer match: everyone is all over the goat.

Another beautiful game is *Kyz Kummai*. The boy on the horse must try to steal a kiss from a girl, also on horseback, while she tries to gallop away from him (unless, of course, she really likes him). You're also guaranteed to see *Oodarysh* during At Chabysh. This is a type of wrestling, but while sitting on a horse; the first man to pull his opponent off the competitor's rearing steed is the winner. In addition to all the horse play, the festival celebrates Kyrgyz culture. Local musicians play on a modest stage, food and beverages are on offer, and local falconers show how well they've trained their impressive birds. Imagine all of this taking place in a tiny settlement of houses in the middle of an endless, desolate plain bordered by snow-topped mountains. This is a festival, far, far away from the rest of the world.

ANNO ORIGIN

The small, strong Kyrgyz horse would have become extinct if a French woman hadn't taken pity on the breed. Now there is even a genuine foundation and a couple of yearly horse festivals to call attention to their plight. There is also a successful breeding program.

PARTICIPATE

You can go horseback riding on a Kyrgyz horse yourself. Almost everywhere in Kyrgyzstan it's possible to arrange expeditions that will last from one day to more. Who knows, the guide might even want to challenge you to a game of Ulak Tartysh?

KYRGYZSTAN

In different locations throughout Kyrgyzstan.

ORIGIN

La Tirana is situated in a mining region that stretches into Bolivia and Peru. The origin of this festival may lay in a yearly celebration, a ritual of the miners, in which they worship Mother Nature.

Fiesta de la Tirana

OVER TWO HUNDRED DANCE GROUPS FROM ALL OVER CHILE GATHER IN A TINY DESERT VILLAGE TO DANCE THROUGH THE DUSTY STREETS DURING LA FIESTA DE LA TIRANA. THEY PERFORM DANCES THAT ARE HUNDREDS OF YEARS OLD, ALL FOR A HOLY VIRGIN WHO WAS ADDED LATER ON.

66

The town of La Tirana does not even boast seven hundred residents, but what this little village does have is a great setup. The plaza in front of the small, simple church is big enough to hold thousands of merrymakers, and the streets are wide and empty, allowing the dance groups to pass through easily, even with their outrageous masks and outfits. On top of that, there's even enough room left to accommodate the thousands of pilgrims and spectators who descend yearly on the town for the festival.

The dance groups, dressed in costumes ranging from the simple to the incredibly elaborate, primarily perform dances whose origins predate the arrival of the Spaniards on the continent. These ancient dances have names like *kalawallos*, *kullacas*, *indios* and *chunchos*. One of the most famous, La Diablada, tells the story of the battle between good and evil which in this dance is represented as the conflict between little devils and the archangel Michael.

The festival is held in honor of Virgin del Carmen, the local patron saint. Praises are sung in her name during mass, her image is carried through the streets, and everyone prays to her for good fortune. The festival is a rich mixture of both old and new beliefs. According to the legend, the town of La Tirana was built on the grave of an Inca princess and her Spanish lover. The princess had escaped after ten thousand Incas from Peru were forced to help seize Chile from the native Indians. The princess built a new, secret life with a group of other escaped Incas, a group to whom she was so bossy she eventually became known as the tyrant, la tirana. When she fell in love with a Spaniard, the Incas couldn't abide it and they shot the love-blinded couple with a volley of arrows. Before she died, she declared that she would go to God because her Spaniard had shown her the truth in time. The village of La Tirana grew on her grave.

The source of this legend was a Catholic Spaniard who was trying to convert the people of this barren northern Chilean region to his faith. The Spaniard claimed that he found a cross near the princess' grave and heard her story directly from God. When the horns and drums disappear from the dusty streets after this yearly festival, the princess and her lover are at peace once more.

Hemingway Days

WEARING SAFARI CLOTHES OR A FISHERMAN'S SWEATER IS RECOMMENDED, BUT SPORTING A GENUINE WHITE BEARD IS ESSENTIAL - FAKE BEARDS WILL NOT BE TOLERATED. DURING THE ANNUAL HEMINGWAY DAYS IN KEY WEST, FLORIDA, THOUSANDS OF ERNEST LOOK-A-LIKES BATTLE FOR THE PRIZED TITLE OF "PAPA."

These merry men travel from all parts of the world to pay homage to the legendary "Papa" Hemingway and to compete to join The Bearded Brotherhood, the exclusive group of previous look-alike contest winners. The Brotherhood is the jury, since many past winners return annually to this island south of Miami where Hemingway resided throughout the 1930s. Hemingway left an enduring legacy in Key West, so, in addition to turning his former home into a museum, the islanders hold this celebration in his honor every July, the month of his birth. In 1981, Sloppy Joe's Bar started the Hemingway look-alike contest. The contest has spawned a week of festivities devoted to Hemingway and his passions. Among many other activities, there's a marlin fishing competition, since the literary giant loved deep-sea fishing, and a road race, since Hemingway was very athletic. For the more intellectuals, there are theatrical competitions and readings.

During the week, the would-be Hemingways must not only accommodate anyone who asks to have photos taken with them, but they must also do their best to impersonate the great man himself, down to the smallest details. That means eating a lot of fish, heavy drinking, and full-belly laughing. Fortunately for the contestants, the writer no longer lived in Key West when he shot himself in the head, so they don't need to recreate that detail.

UNITED STATES

Key West, Florida, USA.

ORIGIN

The writer Ernest Hemingway, also called Papa, lived in Key West during the 1930s and drank at Sloppy Joe's Bar. In 1981, the bar began hosting the Hemingway look-alike competition.

TIPS

The prize for winning the short story competition is $2000.

PARTICIPATE

In addition to watching the bearded men compete in their daily challenges, visitors can wander the streets and stop at the many stalls, drink at Sloppy Joe's, or participate in some of the activities, including fishing, running, wrestling, arm wrestling, and even short story writing. If you'd like to join the look-alike competition, sign up at **www.sloppyjoes.com**. The entire schedule of festival events is at **www.hemingwaydays.net**.

67

68

Festival of the Near-Dead

AFTER A TERRIFYING EXPERIENCE, YOU'VE REALIZED THAT YOUR NUMBER ISN'T UP AND, THANKFULLY, IT'S NOT YOUR TIME YET. YOU'RE NOT DEAD – YOU'VE ONLY HAD A NEAR-DEATH EXPERIENCE. THE BEST WAY TO CELEBRATE YOUR NEW LEASE ON LIFE? COME TO THE SPANISH VILLAGE OF LAS NIEVAS ON JULY 29.

One of the patron saints of this town near the Portuguese border is Santa Marta de Ribarteme, the patron saint of resurrection. Every year on July 29th, all those people from the region who have had a near-death experience in the past year gather together in Las Nievas to thank Santa Marta with a great feast. These grateful individuals honor Santa Marta in an unusual way – by carrying, or riding in, coffins to a special Mass.

At about 10 a.m., the procession begins at the edge of the village and travels on to the church, with the relatives of the near-dead helping to carry the coffins. Thousands of onlookers watch the extraordinary, and somewhat macabre, sight. For those who are unable to fit inside the church, the sermon is played on loudspeakers outside, and is re-broadcast repeatedly throughout the day for anyone who may have missed it. After the Mass, a statue of Santa Marta is paraded through the streets so that everyone can thank her for protecting the near-dead and, perhaps, can also pray for themselves.

It may all seem a bit somber, but although the morning procession is serious, the rest of the day is joyful with a true "fiesta" feeling. Bands play in the squares, filling the town with the sounds of everything from paso dobles to gypsy music. In all directions, there are vendors hawking religious paraphernalia - if you're lucky, you may find that glow-in-the-dark altar you've been looking for. There are countless food stalls offering delicious Galician seafood, particularly squid and octopus. And, of course, wine and beer are plentiful.

Who knows, during all this post-procession craziness, someone just might have a stroke upon hearing the first bang of the fireworks. Naturally, one hopes that he will pull through and get to be one of the coffin-riding celebrants the following year.

SPAIN

Las Nieves, Spain

PARTICIPATE

Everyone can watch the procession and listen to the sermon. After the procession, the celebration with fireworks, drinking and dancing, takes over the streets.

ORIGIN

The Catholic church has never fully permeated this isolated part of Spain. The original festival probably had nothing to do with Santa Marta but rather with the locals' pagan beliefs in witches and exorcising evil spirits. By annexing the Santa Marta element to the festival, the church was likely attempting to integrate Catholic dogma with the locals' pagan beliefs.

Darwin Beer Can Regatta

DRINKING BEER IS EVEN MORE FUN IF YOU CAN FEEL THAT YOU ARE DRINKING FOR A PURPOSE. LIKE THAT YOUR EMPTY BEER CANS COULD BE USED TO BUILD A BOAT! AT THE ANNUAL BEER CAN REGATTA AT MINDIL BEACH IN DARWIN AUSTRALIA, IT'S DRINKING OR DROWNING.

The largest of the Viking-style ships that take part in the Regatta consists of over forty thousand beer cans. The cans' colors have to be coordinated, and each ship's cans are not just fished out of trash bins but are finished by team members. Polishing off all those cans together encourages team spirit. As one team leader put it, "There are fifteen hundred cans in our boat and I am proud to say that we have emptied them together as a team."

Despite the fact that beer is practically worshipped during the day, the Regatta is considered a very family-friendly event. Even the little ones have their own competitions - sailing with home-built ships made out of soda cans, playing tug-of-war, and building sand castles to win prizes.

The highlight of the day is the Battle of Mindil, in which only the largest boats can participate. This isn't a race about speed, but rather a treasure hunt along the ocean's seabed. Using their oars as large water guns and paper bags filled with flour as ammunition, the boats hit the water. In the huge commotion, the boats work to keep their competition from finding the hidden treasure. If the treasure is found, the winning boat is then boarded.

If you're not the overly competitive type, it's no problem. Watching the race from shore means a day on the beach with excellent entertainment, plenty of ice-cold beer and dozens of food stands. Of course, empty cans must be returned at the end of the day.

69

AUSTRALIA

Mindil beach, Darwin, Australia

PARTICIPATE

Well, drinking is a good start. Around nine in the morning you'll need to register your boat at the marked table and pay the entry fee (AU $ 10 for children, AU $ 50 for adult teams). On the Regatta's website an instruction booklet offers boat construction tips. Helpful hints include advice on taping the open side of the cans together to keep water out, and how to best build a catamaran. **www.beercanregatta.org.au**

ORIGIN

Construction workers flown into Darwin to help rebuild the city after a devastating cyclone in 1974 drank so much beer that a waste problem arose. As recycling didn't exist yet, someone suggested something fun to do with all the empty cans, and thus the Beer Can Regatta was born. The local Lions Club organizes the annual festival and its many events and donates the proceeds to charity.

70 Rasta Earth Festival

FEELING DOWN? WHEN YOU WALK AROUND THE RASTA EARTH FESTIVAL YOU WILL CERTAINLY BRIGHTEN UP. IF YOU JOIN THE MEMBERS OF THE CLOSE-KNIT COMMUNITY OF KNYSNA AS THEY CELEBRATE THEIR RASTAFARIAN BELIEFS, YOU'LL GET TO EXPERIENCE A SMALL, WARM MUSIC FESTIVAL FULL OF LOVE. AND IF YOU WISH TO ADD A RELIGIOUS ELEMENT, THE FESTIVAL IS PRECEDED BY A CHURCH MASS.

Shuttle buses, long lines, security checks, watery beer – these are typical attributes of Western pop festivals. There is none of that here at this chilled-out party in southern South Africa. Everything is relaxed at the Rasta Earth Festival. It's all about love, not money. The only law to obey is the law of love - the motto of Brother Max. Brother Max is one of the founding fathers of the House of Judah, the community of Rastafarians living just outside Knysna. The Rasta village was founded in 1993, and today there are about thirty families living there, along a dead-end road.

Throughout the whole year the village is open to tourists; there is even a bed and breakfast on the land. The Rastafarians organize tours for visitors through their village, their houses, their church and their weed plants. They're happy to teach you about their beliefs. The Rastafari movement originated in the 1930s among the poor black population of Jamaica. The movement has its roots in the Old Testament, in the struggle for the emanci-

pation of the black people, and considers Ethiopia the promised land to which every person with African roots will one day return. When Ras Tafari Makonnen was crowned emperor Haile Selassie I of Ethiopia in 1930, the poor Jamaicans rejoiced and came to view him as Jah Rastafari, the second coming of Jesus Christ on earth.

Nature is very important for the Rastas; they eat hardly any meat and prefer unsprayed produce. And alcohol is forbidden, since they believe it's bad for one's health. Marijuana, on the other hand, is seen as perfectly fine, since it brings you closer to Jah. So, at this festival you'll find no beer taps, only soda, and joints are available in abun-

SOUTH AFRICA

Judah Square, Knysna, South Africa.

 PARTICIPATE

Light a joint and let the reggae bring you closer to Jah.

 ORIGIN

The festival celebrates the birthday of Emperor Haile Selassie I on July 23rd as well as Emancipation Day, the end of slavery, on August 1st.

 TIPS

Despite some of their differences from mainstream believers, Rastafarians do prefer that women dress decently when they enter the church and that men remove their hats. Check **www.rastaearthfestival. co.za** for more info.

dance. On a stage that would not be out of place in a flea market in a small village, reggae bands from throughout the region play for an audience made up of Rastafarians from far and wide, as well as reggae lovers and tourists. Most of the visitors come only for the Music Splash, the last two days of the ten-day festival. The main activity of the first week is going to church (but note that women having their period are not welcome at the services). During the Music Splash, you can also visit the church and get a tour through the village. Naturally, throughout the festival you can also find lots of handmade scarves, hats and cellphone holders for sale, all in reggae colors. Not even the Rastafarians can survive only on a diet of love and weed.

71 Canal Parade

GAY PEOPLE LOVE DRESSING UP FOR A GOOD PARTY, AND STRAIGHT PEOPLE LOVE TO ADMIRE THE CREATIVE OUTFITS, SO THE ANNUAL GAY PRIDE CANAL PARADE IN AMSTERDAM IS A WIN-WIN FOR EVERYONE. DOZENS OF BOATS FILLED WITH FABULOUSLY COSTUMED MEN SAIL THROUGH AMSTERDAM'S CANALS TO THE DELIGHT OF THOUSANDS OF SPECTATORS.

Barges full of people pass by, with one group's costumes even wackier than the next: tight pink dresses, pink wigs, and pink feather boas; torsos in leather straps, thick mustaches and lots of body hair. There's lots of air kissing and waving to the crowds, and everyone gets down to the music blasting from speakers on the various boats. But for the participants this event is not just about partying; they are their celebrating their freedom, their pride, and are asking for greater tolerance. The parade has been taking place since 1996, and today it draws hundreds of thousands of specta-tors, including many tourists and families with children. More and more organizations want to get involved with the parade to show that they are gay-friendly. And so you'll see boats sponsored by different ministries, the army, the police, and the Young Christians, to name just a few. That's good for the gay rights movement, of course, but perhaps a bit less of a blessing for the atmosphere of the boat parade. Oh, and in case you are won-dering, the members of the police boat wear their actual police uniforms – not the kinky variation popular in some gay circles.

 NETHERLANDS

Amsterdam, Netherlands.

 PARTICIPATE

The first Amsterdam Gay Pride celebration was organized in 1996 and the boat parade was one of the elements. Despite the low expectations of the organization, the bridges and canal banks were full of people who had come out to witness the spectacle. Since then, the parade has become the most important part of the Gay Pride week.

 ORIGIN

Watching is naturally an option, but a comparatively dull one. Cruising on a boat is more fun. You don't need to be gay to be on the boats; there are plenty of straight people sailing through the canals and enjoying the fes-tive ambiance. You can also arrange your own boat, but it must be done officially. Visit **www.canalparade.nl** to see how.

🌐 FRANCE

Bayonne, France.

⚡ PARTICIPATE

Get into a white/red outfit, tie on a red scarf, and join into the multitudes. Check **www.fetes.bayonne.fr** for the complete schedule. It is possible to participate in the sprints, but make sure to sign up in advance. You'll find more information on the site.

ANNO ORIGIN

The first version of the festivities was called "the big summer festival" and was organized in 1932 by a bunch of friends that knew each other from the local rugby team.

Fêtes de Bayonne

JEALOUSY CAN HAVE ITS BENEFITS. TAKE, FOR INSTANCE, THE FÊTES DE BAYONNE, DURING WHICH TENS OF THOUSANDS OF PEOPLE WALK AROUND WEARING RED SCARVES FOR FIVE DAYS IN A ROW, ONLY BECAUSE THE SAME THING IS DONE IN PAMPLONA. BUT THE BULLS ARE MERELY A SIDE ATTRACTION OF THIS GRAND FRENCH FESTIVAL.

Statues on bridges and rooftops all get a red scarf, too. Not even a dog can leave the house without a scarlet scarf around its neck. The little shawl was one of the first things the citizens of this town in southwestern France copied from Pamplona. That everyone is dressed alike adds to the party. It was in 1932 that the boys from Bayonne were so overcome with jealousy of the festivities taking place in that other little Basque town on the other side of the border that they set out to copy it.

It is almost impossible to give a brief description of the festivities. If pressed, you would have to say that it falls somewhere between a five-day outdoor drinking fest and a dance party. Ten thousand people crowd together in the old streets of the town, all of them clad in white pants, white shirts, and red

ESTA
GATOIRE

shawls. For the Bayonnaise, this is *the* celebration of the year, for the whole family. There is a special area for children where parents can leave their little ones and, with peace of mind, go join some friends to share a bottle of wine in the grass.

Young people wander around during the day, but only at night do they start drinking and flirting in the narrow streets. The days are filled with activities. There's a rowing competition, a soccer game, and, of course, there's a whole lot going on with the bulls. All the while, children are shrieking with both excitement and fear as a mechanical bull passes through the streets. The Basque culture is celebrated with live music, dancing, and delicious food. There are yoga lessons in the plaza, and even fireworks. On one of the afternoons, dolls - giant dolls, in fact - are lifted through the streets. This last element was also copied, not from Pamplona but from the *Fêtes de Gayant (Giant Festival)* in Douai. But, really, how much does originality matter when you are having so much fun?

72

Maralal Camel Derby

DROMEDARIES ARE STUBBORN AND UNPREDICTABLE, DECIDING EXACTLY HOW FAST THEY WILL GO WHILE CARRYING THEIR TOURIST PASSENGERS TO THE FINISH LINE, TEN KILOMETERS AWAY. IT'S NOT WISE TO PARTICIPATE IN THE MARALAL CAMEL DERBY IF YOU CAN'T STAND LOSING. YOUR FATE LIES IN THE HOOVES OF YOUR FURRY PARTNER, AND THE ONLY THING YOU CAN DO IS BOBBLE ALONG ON THE RIGHT RHYTHM.

KENYA

Maralal, Kenya

....

PARTICIPATE

Go the day before the race to the Yare Camel Club to sign up and get set up with your dromedary. The owner or driver will also be provided. He will help you get on, will set the dromedary up on the start line, and will encourage the animal. Animal lovers who find it difficult to see an animal beaten, especially if it is for your own pleasure, may want to only watch the race. The dromedaries are often beaten and pulled by ropes to keep them under control, and they can roar very loudly if there is something they dislike.

....

ORIGIN

The Maralal camel derby has been running since 1990. The race was intended to boost the local economy, and it worked. The festival attracts many drivers from different countries in the region as well as tourists from all over the world. The derby also provides an ideal opportunity to raise awareness about the causes and consequences of the continual desertification of this region.

....

....

The dromedary camel traces its origins to northern Kenya but has spread over the centuries to many other countries. During the three days of the Camel Derby, professional camel drivers as well as novices, tourists, and spectators, return to the camel's birthplace and fill the dusty northern Kenyan town of Maralal with excitement and energy. Professional drivers compete in a hotly-contested race of 42 kilometers (around 26 miles). Only those in perfect control of their dromedaries and who are able to keep the animal at full speed - an impressive 40 kph - will have a chance at the prize, which consists mainly of glory and great respect within the community.

During the days of the derby, the sleepy town of Maralal comes alive. Merchandise and food vendors are everywhere, and traditionally-dressed Samburu women come from miles around to dance and giggle at all the funny *mzungus* (foreigners) attempting to ride the camels. In addition to the ten kilometer race, the mzungus can also try their luck at the tri-camel-thon. This entails a bit of running, cycling, and then a camel race. Chances are, though, if you do choose to participate, you'll be competing against locals as well. Thus the likelihood of you losing increases along with the hysterics of the spectators lining the roadsides. View it as a sort of sustainable tourism – you come to entertain yourself, and in return you provide the locals with enough laughs to last until next year's race.

A chemical toilet in the dark ages? No, when you 'had to go' a thousand years ago, you just went to the open sewers

74 Medeltidsveckan

TAAATAAAAA! THE TOWN CRIER ANNOUNCES THAT MEDELTIDSVECKAN HAS STARTED! HUNDREDS OF THOUSANDS OF PEOPLE HAVE INVADED THE ANCIENT TOWN OF VISBY, ON THE ISLAND OF GOTLAND IN SWEDEN, AND ARE READY TO RELIVE MEDIEVAL LIFE FOR A WEEK.

For Medieval Week, Visby is removed from modernity - not too difficult, perhaps, since it's an isolated place with over 200 medieval houses still standing and plenty of ruins. Walking through the narrow, winding streets, or around the ramparts, it's easy to feel transported back to the days of Robin Hood, crusades, robbers, and knights. The brutal side of the Middle Ages – mass killings, rape, disease – is conveniently not celebrated during this festival. Medeltidsveckan is, after all, a family event, not to mention the annual fix for history junkies who like to dress up.

These history enthusiasts from all over Europe, and beyond, take their hobby very seriously and truly behave as if they are back in the Middle Ages, down to almost every detail. They've carefully recreated the clothing, learned the right words, and know which tools to use. During the archery tournament, you will see evidence of this: hardly anyone is doing this for the first time.

The old town is abuzz with activity. Troubadours recite ancient lyric poems and love stories to whoever passes by. Children are entertained by men with

SWEDEN

Visby, Gotland, Sweden.

 PARTICIPATE

Dress as a medieval person and automatically become a member of this secret society. Make sure to come equipped with the proper clothing, from a simple tunic to an expensive chainmail knight's outfit. Workshops - from history lessons to archery – take place during the week, for those who really want to learn more about the time period. If you're feeling particularly eager, you can also volunteer to carry the flags in the stadium during the jousting tournament. Find more details about it all at **www.medeltidsveckan.se.**

 ORIGIN

During the Middle Ages, Visby was one of the important Hanseatic towns, evidence of which is still visible today. There are still 200 houses within the walled medieval town. It was declared a UNESCO World Heritage Site in 1995. Medeltidsveckan has been organized since 1984.

fake beards, jugglers, and jokers trying hard today to earn a few coins. Perhaps you'd like to buy a souvenir of your time travel?. A beautiful handmade cape, maybe? A painting? Or perhaps a wooden chalice?

The most spectacular event of the week may be the jousting competition in the stadium. With beautifully decorated steeds, dressed in chainmail and protected by shields, the knights attack each other with lances. Naturally, each knight has his own detailed biography so the audience can learn a bit more about these brave men in armor. For instance, Lyckans Riddare is always lucky – he went on a crusade and survived without a scratch. Women take part in their own competitions, with crossbows. Sometimes an apple is the target, or sometimes it's a wooden duck. It may look easy, but come try it for yourself. And make sure to dress appropriately, since these history buffs will call you out on it if you don't.

La Regate des Baignoires

YOU'RE NOT LIKELY TO ACTUALLY SEE ANY BATHTUBS DURING THE BELGIAN BATHTUB REGATTA. THAT'S BECAUSE THEY ARE HIDDEN UNDER HUGE, CREATIVE CONSTRUCTIONS OF CARDBOARD LEFFE BEER BOTTLES, WATERSLIDES, PIRATE SHIPS, AND TRAYS FULL OF LITTLE BLUE SMURFS. BUT REST ASSURED THAT THE JUDGES DO CHECK BEFORE EACH RAFT HITS THE WATER. NO BATHTUB UNDER YOUR VESSEL? NO SAILING FOR YOU!

There is a prize for the fastest craft. No, fastest is not really the right word... There is a prize for the craft that arrives at the finish line first. This race is definitely not about speed. La Régate des Baignoires moves at a snail's pace, since it's quite a feat to paddle an unwieldy, bathtub-bottomed vessel against the current of the Meuse River. During the voyage, the cowboy raft carrying the bachelor party might catch the eye of the girls on the butcher's boat, but it is forbidden to board another floating craft. Throwing buckets of water at each other, however, is allowed. This raises the stakes both on the water and along the riverbanks.

On the same riverbanks, when the weather allows it, the residents of Dinant fold open their lawn chairs, build extra terraces, and let the cold beer flow steadily through the taps. Behind them, the steep stone cliffs rise up in the air, creating a truly stunning and dramatic setting. This beautiful town, however, was plagued for centuries by suffering. Louis XI and Charles the Bold both used the town as a battleground. In fact, in the very river where this wild festival now takes place, Charles the Bold had 800 of the town's residents tied up and pushed into the water, killing them all.

But the harsh times are all but forgotten during the revelry of the modern "battle." The bathtub skirmish in the water was, at its beginning, all about money. In the early 1980s, the tourist agency of Dinant wanted to increase tourism by doing something to generate excitement about the town; it's clear that they've succeeded. At first, mostly only the local business owners participated. The baker, the butcher, restaurant and bar owners all dragged their own bathtubs into the water in the hopes of achieving victory. You can still see the locals participating today. And those entrants who decorate their ships in a theme that references the town of Dinant can count on extra points from the jury. The jury also thinks highly of themes that incorporate current events, not to mention, of course, originality and attractiveness. But don't focus only on the design of the bathtub ship itself; also keep the sailors in mind. The stranger the outfits of the crew, the better. The fact that your outfit will probably cross the finish line completely drenched won't affect your score.

BELGIUM

Dinant, Belgium.

Since 1982

PARTICIPATE

Paddling a bathtub down the Meuse River on a summer's day, life can't get more relaxed than that, right? The tricky part is getting your bathtub ship to Dinant. One solution is to arrange a bathtub in Dinant a few days in advance and remodel it on the spot. You can sign up for the regatta through **lesbaignoires.jimdo.com**, or in person up to a couple of hours before the race.

TIPS

⚡ Are you a music lover? Then keep in mind that Adolphe Sax, the inventor of the saxophone was born in 1814 in Dinant. His house is now a museum.

⚡ Also, for treasure hunters, during La Régate des Baignoires there is always a flea market alongside the shore.

Tetsuya Odori

ALL-NIGHTERS. THE JAPANESE PRACTICALLY INVENTED THEM. NOT BOUNCING TO TRANCE MUSIC, BUT MOVING GRACEFULLY UNDER THE STARS, ALL NIGHT LONG, IN KIMONOS. CLAPPING THEIR HANDS FOR HOURS AND DANCING IN WOODEN SANDALS TO WELCOME THE SPIRITS BACK TO EARTH.

For three nights in August, the Japanese dance through the streets all night long, from eight in the evening until five in the morning. All lined up, one behind the other, they all do the exact same dance, like one big, elegant flash mob. Their arms flutter to the right, to the left, clap, clap! Old ladies in kimonos, young girls in hip skirts, old men in glasses, boys in sneakers... during Tetsuya Odori in Gujo Hachiman, everyone dances together. Tetsuya Odori (Nightly Dance) is a part of Bon Odori (Summer Dance), the period of thirty summer nights during which the Japanese dance in the evenings. Each region has its own dances, which are fairly simple and consist of endless repetitions of a few steps. They are easy to learn so that everyone can participate - even tourists, who are encouraged to join in. Everyone steps, claps, and dances together to welcome the spirits of their ancestors, which was the original intention of Bon Odori and Tetsuya Odori.

In the quaint town of Gujo Hachiman, located in a pristine valley in the mountains, the dance marathons are celebrated with particular enthusiasm. Musicians are driven through the streets on wooden floats, and amplifiers ensure that the dancers, who are a hundred meters farther away, can still maintain the rhythm of the traditional Japanese music.

But this dancing, regardless of how perfect and devoted the participants may be, is not an arduous business. It's instead an experience of pure joy. There are even old-fashioned block parties in which people dance under paper lanterns and the stars. The physical exhaustion from the dancing, combined with the fresh mountain air and the cozy community feeling, can transport you to a state of blissful ecstasy. There is no more satisfying way to roll into bed.

 JAPAN

Gujo Hachiman, Japan.

 PARTICIPATE

If you're not even capable of following along during aerobics class, you should definitely prepare during the dance workshops for tourists that are organized in Gujo Hachiman during the days of the festival.

 ORIGIN

Over four hundred years ago, the master of the region around Gujo Hachiman encouraged the inhabitants to celebrate together in the open air, because it fostered a sense of community. And they still do the same today.

 TIPS

You can simply participate in your western attire, but if you want to go all-out Japanese, rent a modest cotton kimono (yukata) and wooden slippers (geta) from one of the stands on the street.

76

"JAMBO"
FOR SAFETY......
SWIM BETWEEN THE FLAGS

Henley on Todd Regatta

THE ANNUAL REGATTA IN ARID, SWELTERING ALICE SPRINGS IS MAYBE THE ONLY BOAT RACE YOU CAN FIND WHERE NO WATER IS IN SIGHT. SINCE ALICE SPRINGS IS 1.500 KILOMETERS FROM THE NEAREST LARGE BODY OF WATER, THE BIZARRE, SELF-MADE BOAT STRUCTURES IN THIS RACE COMPETE ON THE ARID RIVERBED OF THE TODD RIVER.

AUSTRALIA

Alice Springs, in the heart of Australia.

ORIGIN

In 1962 Reg Smith came up with the idea for the regatta, inspired, of course, by the chic and prestigious upper-class British regatta Henley-on-Thames. Australians enjoy poking a bit of fun at their English cousins. The local Rotary clubs sponsor the event and collect money for charity.

TIPS

Some hostels have teams that guests can join. You can also help to build the boat.

PARTICIPATE

The entry fee is twelve dollars for Australian adults, five for children. Should you want to enter a boat race, you'll need to create you own bottomless boat. Full-on participation is obviously the best option, so come a few days before the regatta to Alice Springs and build your boat, decorate it, and get it all pimped out and ready to race.

On one occasion, the event had to be canceled, since there was an unexpected natural phenomenon that affected the riverbed: rainwater. And racing on water is not the intention of this boat race. During Henley-on-Todd, men do the leg work and the only water in sight is the sweat dripping from their faces.

In an ironic nod to their rowing counterparts at that other famous Henley – you know, the one on the Thames – these heroic racers compete in bottomless "eights," yachts, and even bath tubs, through the deep sand of this riverbed. Unlike at that other, more fancy regatta in England, costumes are of great importance to these racers; Viking and Pirate themes abound. Other sights you might not get to see every day include a submersible vehicle being paddled forward through the sand, and a relay involving competitors rolling along the river bed in man-sized hamster wheels. There are companies that participate and decorate their craft with banners, and of course there are teams celebrating birthday parties, bachelor parties, and even groups of backpackers who've just met each other that morning.

Should you take part informally, you can always join the fun and get in on the big joke in another way. Everywhere you'll find water guns, water tanks, water balloons, and even signs along the riverbed declaring "No Fishing."

Damascus is the oldest continuously inhabited city in the world. It is now Islamic but is considered to be the origin of Christian Society.

Eid al-Fitr

LICK YOUR LIPS FOR THE SANDY DATE COOKIE, OPEN YOUR MOUTH FOR A DELICIOUS PIECE OF BAKLAVA, DRIPPING WITH HONEY. DURING EID AL-FITR, CELEBRATING THE END OF RAMADAN, THE SOUKS ARE FILLED TO THE BRIM WITH SWEETS. IT'S THREE DAYS OF UNRESTRAINED EATING!

The charming old souks of Damascus become a candy paradise during the feasting days of Eid al-Fitr. Everyone goes out into the streets to stock up on and eat sweets, and to listen to music and occasionally dance together. The exuberant atmosphere and the feeling of togetherness is perhaps akin to New Year's Eve in other countries. The merrymakers have just finished observing Ramadan, the Islamic month of fasting. With this celebration, sometimes referred to as *sugar feast* in other languages, the believers are returning to their normal lives.

The celebration of Eid al-Fitr takes place all over the world, wherever Muslims live, but it is especially lively in Damascus, where the streets are filled with people and there is a carnival atmosphere. The market stands, already a lovely sight with their bags full of spices, neatly stacked vegetables, and waterfalls of shoes and scarves, are decorated even more beautifully for the Eid celebration. Bakers work themselves to the bone to produce enough powdered sugar-topped almond delights, nougat cubes, and pistachio cook-

78

ies to feed the hungry masses, and they stack them like works of art. Musicians and other entertainers add to the joyous holiday feeling. Everyone shows up in the streets in their best, and often new, party clothes – long, dazzling colored outfits. They wish each other happiness and celebrate having endured the difficult month of fasting and thereby proven their loyalty to Allah. But you don't need to be able to claim the same thing in order to enjoy a bag of date cookies.

 SYRIA

Damascus, Syria. (And all over the world where Muslims live).

....

....

 **ORIGIN**

During the ninth month of the Islamic calendar, the content of the Koran was shown to Mohammed. During that month (Ramadan), Muslims must fast. As soon as the new month starts, and therefore the new moon is visible, Eid al-Fitr begins. This is not the same day everywhere in the world; high priests determine if the new moon has appeared in the right way or not and, therefore, whether Ramadan is over.

....

Bog Snorkeling

INHALING MUD THROUGH YOUR SNORKEL, YOUR VISION OBSCURED BY MUDDY WATER. THERE ARE CERTAINLY BETTER PLACES FOR SNORKELING THAN A TRENCH CUT OUT OF A PEAT BOG NEAR THE WELSH VILLAGE WITH THE UNPRONOUNCEABLE NAME OF LLANWRTYD WELLS.

To add to the degree of difficulty, you also can't use conventional swimming strokes in this competition. You must rely only on the power of your flippers to swim the two laps of about 60 meters each. Oh, and even though it's late August, it can be downright chilly outside and in the trench (think rain, wind, ten degree temperatures). This is England after all. Or, rather, Wales. It's logical, then, that many participants, men and women alike, compete in wetsuits. Others may sport interesting attire: a Buzz Lightyear costume, a couple of horse outfits, an inflatable Sumo wrestler disguise, and more

🌐 WALES

In a meadow near Llan-wrtyd Wells, Wales, UK.

🔖 ORIGIN

Bog snorkeling has been organized since 1985.

👍 TIPS

Compete either for speed or for the best costume.
Put on a wetsuit if it's cold, so that your muscles don't freeze up in those chilly waters.
Make sure your car or trailer is equipped with warm towels, dry clothes, and hot drinks for afterwards.

⚡ PARTICIPATE

If you are over fourteen, you may participate. Not only are there prizes for the fastest overall swimmer, but also for the fastest in various categories (Women, Juniors, etc). To participate costs fifteen pounds, which goes to charity. A registration form and more info are available at **www.green-events.co.uk.** Women are only required to swim one lap, so they've only got to slog it out for 60 meters.

in that vein. The best-dressed snorkeler gets a prize. As does the person who spends the longest time splashing around in the mud. You may pity that poor soul, but perhaps he's onto something; after all, in the 18th century, people flocked to the medicinal mud baths of this tiny town.
The idea for the event was generated by some local men in 1985 in an effort to generate revenue for Llanwrtyd Wells, Great Britain's smallest town. The event has been successful enough to spawn spin-offs, the Mountain Bike Bog Snorkeling Championship and the Bog Snorkeling Triathlon. Similar events also take place in Australia and Ireland, inspired by this wacky tradition. But for the *original experience* you need to come to this muddy ditch in Wales.

La Tomatina

SPLAT! A SLIMY, ROTTEN TOMATO HITS YOU RIGHT IN THE CHEST. AND WHEN YOU REFILL YOUR SUPPLY OF TOMATO AMMUNITION FROM THE COBBLESTONE STREETS, YOU GET A DIRECT HIT ON YOUR BOTTOM. NO WONDER THE AUTHORITIES ADVISE ANYONE PARTICIPATING IN LA TOMATINA – THE TOMATO FESTIVAL – TO STRONGLY CONSIDER WEARING PROTECTIVE GOGGLES.

For exactly one hour, fifty thousand people pelt each other with crushed tomatoes (the tomatoes are squished to reduce the risk of injury to the participants). Over one hundred tons of tomatos are thrown during this hour of red chaos. This annual summer event in Buñol, a village just west of Valencia in Spain, has become world famous and spawned imitations across the globe, but the real thing happens only here. Only nine thousand people live in and around Buñol, a town filled with old buildings and streets paved with smooth cobblestones . Every last Wednesday of August,

the residents and shopkeepers in the center of town board up their houses and stores to protect themselves from the imminent tomato brawl. Early on the morning of the event, truckloads of specially grown, cheap tomatoes from Extremadura are brought into town. At eleven a.m., a ham is placed atop a greased pole. The tomato war can only begin after someone has climbed the pole and brought down the ham. Once that happens, tomato fury is unleashed. Volunteers manning trucks filled with tomatoes arm the participants, filling their eager hands with squishy, red am-

munition. Everyone grabs as much as he can and throws it at anything that moves.

And then, one hour later, the world's largest vegetable fight is all over and it's time to start the hosing down. Fire engines replace the tomato convoy, spraying and showering the masses. Residents living on the upper floors of buildings may even open their windows to soak the festival-goers with a bucket of water or perhaps spray them down with a garden hose. Some people even take a plunge in the nearby river in an attempt to cleanse themselves of the stinking mess.

80

🌐 SPAIN

Buñol, Spain.

⚡ RULES

⚡ Squish your tomatoes before you throw them.
⚡ Step aside for slow-moving vehicles – not out of courtesy, but self-preservation.
⚡ Stop when the cannon fires.

⚙ ORIGIN

The origins of La Tomatina are unclear. One theory has it that, sometime in 1944 or 1945, two groups of youths started fighting in the food market. Another guess is that disgruntled youths pelted local politicians with tomatoes during an official parade. Yet another theory holds that an accident involving a truckload of tomatoes led to a spontaneous celebration.

⚡ PARTICIPATE

Watching without participating is not an option.

👍 TIPS

⚡ The night before La Tomatina, there is a market with a fair and a festival.
⚡ If you really want to be at the epicenter of the festivities, on the morning of the event make sure you are in the village square at least eight hours prior to the start.
⚡ Leave your children at home, since there is no way you can protect them from the tomato chaos.
⚡ Take only a waterproof camera.

☠ 🐦 🐍 🍺

Air Guitar Festival

THEY'VE BORROWED THE POINT SYSTEM OF ICE SKATING AND THE AESTHETICS OF THE GLAM ROCKERS AND THROWN IN AN ELEMENT OF PRIMAL MALE COMPETITIVENESS. WHAT LIVING ROOM ROCKER COULD POSSIBLY STAY CALM UPON HEARING AN AMAZING SOLO LIKE THIS?

During this yearly championship, the best air guitarists in the world compete against each other. Japan, Australia, America, England and The Netherlands are always represented. The participants have names like Tremolo Theer, Mr. Magic, and Günther Love, and they sport tiger-print leggings, leather pants with strategic missing pieces, and gold latex pantyhose. You'll also see many bare torsos, gold chains, ripped T-shirts, and leather jackets. The hair style of choice is, naturally, long and curly, so as to be best swung around, since there is more to this contest than moving your fingers; the jury also gives points for the overall performance.

Of course, the performance must be technically accurate – whatever is mimed is what should be heard. If the guitar stops in the music and the rocker is still playing some notes, he's a worthless air guitarist. Podium performance is the second point of attention: charisma and playing to the crowd are crucial. And, of course, there are strict rules. You can dress up, but it's forbidden to take an entourage with you on stage. You have to play the air guitar, but you cannot play another air instrument. The third category on which the five headed jury judges is *airness*, the art of air guitaring. This may be as subjective and intangible as the guitars themselves, but what is a championship without a bit of arguing with the jury?

⚡ PARTICIPATE

Everyone can participate in the qualifying rounds. The final is strictly for the cream of the crop. To be among them, practice, practice, practice! Hire a coach, make time for hours of training, find a stylist, and arrange the choreography that will best display your most amazing tricks –head banging, emotional solos, and playing the guitar close to the ground.

🌐 FINLAND

Oulu, Finland.

ANNO ORIGIN

The air guitar has likely been played since the invention of the guitar, and perhaps even earlier. In the 1980s, the first organized contests were held. In 1996, the Oulu Music Video Festival organized a small air guitar competition as a joke, since they had an empty spot in the program. Since then, it's become the biggest and most important air guitar festival in the world and now draws more attention than the Music Video Festival itself.

👍 TIPS

Check **www.airguitarworld-championships.com** to learn everything about the final in Oulu.

Twenty countries fight for a place in the finals, and that number is growing every year. All the finalists (and their groupies, naturally) travel to the finnish town of Oulu. In the town's marketplace, there is a huge stage, befitting true rock stars. An enormous set of speakers blasts music to the crowd of a thousand spectators, and a lightshow rounds out the performance.

The contest consists of two rounds. First, the candidates must air guitar for one minute to music of their choice. This is all about studied choreography – the air guitarist can make his guitar scream at just the right moment and can jump in the air during his epic solo. The second round is the improvisation round in which the player is given an unknown song to which he must mime. The first round is spectacular due to the performance element, the second because of the sheer excitement. Will he miss a note? Does he put his guitar in his neck?

According to the organization, the only goal of this contest is to promote world peace. The belief is that the evil will vanish in the world if everyone plays the air guitar. To this end, at the culmination of the contest final, all the spectators raise their hands in the air as one.

Cowal
Highland Gathering

LIKE HULK HOGAN THE ATHLETES OF THESE HIGHLAND GAMES FLEX THEIR MUSCLES IN FRONT OF CHEERING CROWDS AND GRUNT NOISILY AS THEY HOIST TREE TRUNKS AND BOULDERS OFF THE GROUND. A COMPETITION OF STRENGTH NEED NOT BE DEVOID OF HUMOR.

The largest Highland Games competition in the world, the Cowal Gathering takes place in a meadow in Dunoon, just west of Glasgow. On this field, athletes from around the world come together to measure up against each other by the standards of ancient Scottish and Celtic tradition. These heavyweights try to outdo each other in such events as the Scottish hammer throw, the weight toss, the stone put and, of course, the caber toss (the caber being a long pine pole or log).

The goal of the caber toss is not to throw the log a great distance but rather to try to flip it 180 degrees. With a pole three times your own size, this is quite a task. The winner is the athlete whose pole points closest to twelve o'clock, or perpendicular to the ground.

Along with the male powerhouses – clad in kilts, naturally – are heavyweight women competitors, who throw, swing and grunt just like the guys. Yet the Cowal Gathering is not about brute strength alone; competitors must also possess a certain level of grace to succeed.

The Gathering is also the premier competition for Highland dancers and pipe bands. Each year, about six hundred Highland dancers, even as young as eight years old, can be seen flopping their tartan-socked legs in the air while doing an old Scottish fling or sword. For the newly initiated, this medieval form of dancing can at first seem cute, but it's a deadly serious competition for the members of this dancing subculture that spans the world.

The same is true for the pipe bands. Bagpipe players come from far and wide to prove that their band is the best. The highlight of this part of the festival, according to the festival's organizer, is when all the bands come together to play the laddie. Indeed, the sound of 2.500 bagpipes and drums playing at once is unforgettable.

82

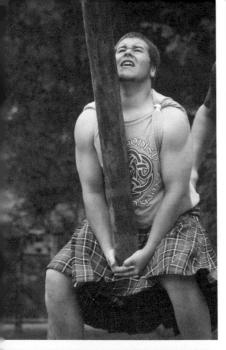

SCOTLAND

Dunoon, Scotland

PARTICIPATE

Train really hard. Or, just buy a ticket and watch the competition. Tickets can be easily purchased the day of the event. Each ticket costs only a couple of pounds. Another alternative is to participate in the five kilometer footrace. It's certainly easier than the caber toss. Visit **www.cowalgathering. com** for more info.

ANNO ORIGIN

The Cowal Gathering was first held in 1894, with the heavyweight competition forming the basis of the event. The bagpipe competition was added in 1906, but the dancing competition only began in 2003.

Umhlanga

THE ULTIMATE MENS DREAM? THAT WOULD
BE 15.000 VIRGINS GATHER EVERY YEAR ON
A PLAIN IN SWAZILAND. CLAD IN JUST A FEW
TRADITIONAL PIECES OF CLOTH AND BEADS,
AND DANCE FOR THE KING. AFTER ALL, HE
JUST MIGHT PICK A NEW WIFE FROM THEIR
MIDST.

Every year, young women come from all corners of this tiny country to honor
the queen mother, who rules alongside the king. The whole festival lasts
eight days, and it reaches its climax when the virgins offer their freshly-cut
reed stems to the queen mother.

More than two hundred tribes participate, and each girl wears a sash denot-
ing her tribe during the most important parts of Umhlanga. On the second
day, the virgins are divided into two groups, the really young ones (between
8 and 14) and the slightly older ones (between 14 and 22). The really young
girls walk to a reed field about 10 kilometers away to find their offerings,
while the older group must undertake a journey of 30 kilometers. There they
chop the reed to offer to the queen mother on the sixth day.

 SWAZILAND

Swaziland, in the hometown of the reigning queen mother, currently Ludzidzini.

 PARTICIPATE

On the sixth and seventh days, you can see the young women do the traditional dances wearing over 200 different kinds of garments. Are you a more hands-on type of guy? Then you can always propose to one of the girls, but make sure you don't do that directly to the girl. You'll need to go to the leader of her tribe to ask permission.

One of the reasons for the massive gathering is to promote chastity, so Umhlanga is not a sex romp for the Swazi men. This does not mean, however, that men cannot compete for the women's hands during the festival. Quite the opposite, actually. During Umhlanga, bachelors camp out in the surrounding areas to check out the ladies and perhaps start the negotiations with the family of a charming girl, since a virgin is never given away for free.

The king can also make his choice during the sixth and seventh days, the real highlight of the festival. That is the moment when all the girls dance for the king and the queen mother in their traditional tribal attire (here and there with a mobile phone on a key cord, dangling between bare breasts). The last king never skipped a year. The current king, Mswati III, is a Christian and only chooses a new bride every now and then.

On the last day of the festival, cows are slaughtered, at the expense of the king. Every girl who does not end up going home with the king can take a piece of fresh meat back to her village.

83

Burning Man

IF YOU WANT TO RUN AROUND IN THE DESERT FOR EIGHT DAYS WEARING NOTHING BUT A THONG AND A WINDMILL ON YOUR HEAD, *GOOD FOR YOU!* BURNING MAN IS ALL ABOUT SELF-EXPRESSION – LET THE CREATIVE PART OF YOU THAT REMAINS HIDDEN IN YOUR DAILY LIFE BREAK THROUGH!

Heat, isolation, altitude, sand storms... these demanding desert circumstances should help you to achieve a hallucinatory state of mind, even without the stimulating drugs. To see bizarre shapes, monsters, and animals, you don't need any pharmaceuticals at all; the fantasy world is all around and you are a part of it. There are no spectators at Burning Man: each *burner* is a participant and each burner makes the festival what it is. The inhabitants of this town that exists eight days a year build the community themselves – every person has creative input. While the biggest and most impressive pieces of art at the festival are built in advance by artists who are compensated for their work, each burner is himself a work of art. Someone is dressed in a futuristic stilt costume; another is wearing a suit made of light sticks; someone else carries a children's slide; another holds a treasure chest that is filled with disguises. Creativity is everywhere.

While almost anything is possible and allowed during Burning Man, there are some key principles. Voyeurs, naturally, are not appreciated, since it is all about participating and not watching. Everyone needs to be self-providing – you have to take your own food, drinks, and sunscreen and any other necessities that you will need for the eight day festival. Moreover, the Leave No Trace policy by which burners must abide means that you truly cannot leave anything behind, not even dishwater. Also, money will do you no good at Burning Man; a *gifting economy* is promoted, and this is all about giving without expecting anything in return. Mutual trade is forbidden and you can only use your dollars for gasoline and popsicles. The temporary desert town of Black Rock City – tens of thousands strong – is built in a half-moon shape around *The Man*, a twenty-meter-high statue. On the seventh night, when everyone is pleasantly worn out, the event reaches its climax: The Man is lit on fire. The burning is a symbol of merging, as well as a celebration of rebirth. It can also symbolize something special and personal to you. Because, as much as Burning Man is about community, it is also profoundly personal and about your individual experience.

SEP

THE WEEK PRIOR TO LABOR DAY, (THE FIRST MONDAY IN SEPTEMBER). THE MAN IS SET ABLAZE ON SATURDAY EVENING.

 UNITED STATES

Black Rock Desert, Nevada, United States.

 ORIGIN

Burning Man started out as a solstice celebration on a beach near San Francisco. In 1986, Larry Harvey built a three-meter-high man to set on fire, a ritual that a buddy of his had earlier abandoned. Larry called the burning of the man a spontaneous form of self-expression. He made it a yearly tradition until the police prohibited it in 1990. The man was broken up into pieces and transported to another festival in the Nevada desert, where it was set ablaze. Since then, Burning Man has been organized in the Black Rock Desert and is now held at the end of August rather than during the solstice.

 TICKETS

Check **www.burningman.com**. Tickets get more expensive as the festival gets closer; you should expect to pay about $250.

 TIPS

- People will be checking at the gate whether the burners have enough food and water to stay alive for the eight days. You will be sent back if you don't have enough - 5.7 liters (1.5 American gallons) are mandatory per person, per day.
- Black Rock is, in addition to being a desert, also at a very high altitude. So it's hot during the day but quite chilly at night. Packing a comfortable sweater is a wise move.
- Take a bike with you, with lights, so you can travel the long distances of the festival terrain day or night.

DICTIONARY

- **MOOP:** Matter Out Of Place. Waste.
- **Obtainium:** Any useful and valued material which is found or obtained for free.
- **Playa Foot:** A foot that has become so dried out by the desert air and ground that it cracks.

Algemesi, Spain

ORIGIN

La Muixeranga is believed to have begun hundreds of years ago with a group of Moorish 'show offs'. In the many years since the time of the Moors, the towers have become bigger and much more spectacular. The religious element was not part of the festival in the beginning; it was added later when the Catholic church appropriated the tradition and attached a virgin saint to it.

PARTICIPATE

Looking on in amazement is likely all you'll be doing during La Muixeranga. But if you want to be in a tower yourself, you can contact the human tower group Nova Muixeranga (www.novamuxeranga.com). This group has emerged as the caretaker of this cultural tradition and would be more than happy to help others experience this event.

85 La Muixeranga

ONE FOOT ON A SHAKY SHOULDER, THE OTHER SHIVERING IN THE WIND, THE CHILD HAS TO STAND ON TOP OF SIX OTHER PEOPLE. ONLY WHEN HE REACHES THE TOP IS THE HUMAN TOWER COMPLETE, AND THE CHILD CAN SLIDE BACK DOWN TO THE GROUND.

La Muixeranga is the collective name for a variety of ancient acrobatic dances and human castles that are performed in honor of the Virgen de la Salud, or the Virgin of Health, in Algemesi, near Valencia. The groups practice year-round to create the complicated human structures. These human *castelles* (towers, in Catalan) are built in other cities in Catalonia as well. But it is only in Algemesi that the inhabitants build themselves into towers alongside people performing traditional dances. For the largest, highest and most solid of the towers, around 200 people are needed. Only recently have women been able to join in. Men always form the base, and there are also people who function as living mattresses – in case someone should tumble off the tower. The finished living statues are supposed to be representations of religious or pagan themes with names like "the

altar", "the mulberry tree" and "the funeral" – although you probably won't be able to deduce a particular form.

Everyone involved wears bright, colorful harlequin-style suits and white dance shoes. During the 'construction' process, a piercing bagpipe-like instrument pierces the air with a familiar melody- this same tune has been played for hundreds of years, and was even unsuccessfully offered as Valencia's regional anthem.

During the construction of over five hundred human towers, spectators parade through the streets. They very politely give the *castellers* room, hoping a child doesn't lose his balance and tumble to the ground as the human castle reaches its highest point. Also, as this is a religious festival in Spain, it goes without saying that there are plenty of tapas and drinks on offer, too.

Sukkot

IN THESE HECTIC AND STRESSFUL TIMES, IT CAN BE FUN TO BEHAVE LIKE A CHILD EVERY NOW AND THEN. AND WHAT BETTER WAY TO DO THAT THAN BY BUILDING – AND LIVING IN – HUTS? DURING THE HOLIDAY OF SUKKOT, MANY ISRAELIS LIVE OUTDOORS IN HUTS FOR A FULL WEEK. THEY DO THIS TO COMMEMORATE THE SIMPLE DWELLINGS IN WHICH THE ANCIENT ISRAELITES LIVED DURING THEIR FORTY YEARS OF EXILE IN THE DESERT.

The structures can sometimes be in the middle of the street; it's not a problem. No building permits are required; you can just build *sukkah* (huts) near your house, pretty much wherever you feel like it. But of course the structures are only temporary, up only for the seven festive days. For many Jewish people, Sukkot is an intimate family event. Families and communities build and decorate huts together. It's common to put knickknacks on the walls and lights on the ceiling. The purpose is to eat and spend time in the hut for a week to celebrate and remember the ancient Israelites and their journey. It was the sukkah that sheltered the roaming people from the elements.

It wouldn't be a religious celebration without a few rules, and Sukkot has many. Just building any hut you can dream up is not an option. The huts must meet certain specifications. The roof must be made of natural materials that are no longer attached to their sources (so branches or leaves must have already been detached from their trees or bushes). The roof has to be directly under the blue sky; if your hut is covered by a canopy, that won't fly. For the sides of the cabin any material can be used, but the sides cannot bend in the wind.

The rules can be cumbersome and confusing, and an entire industry has sprung up just to simplify things. These days, you can just buy your hut at the local home improvement store, in all shapes and forms. It's less like building a cabin now and more like pitching a tent. The only problem that remains is that of the rooftops, which are made out of natural items. Many people venture into the woods or go to the park to gather (or chop down) some branches, to the great displeasure of nature lovers who would prefer that everyone buy their materials in a shop or at one of the stands that sell certified materials alongside the road.

Another important element in the hut is the presence of four specific herbs: myrrh twigs, willow twigs, branches of the palm tree, and citrus fruit. The

SEP

FROM THE 15TH TILL THE 21ST
DAY OF THE JEWISH MONTH
TISREI, SEPTEMBER/OCTOBER.

 ISRAEL

Jerusalem, Israel (and the rest of the country).

....

 ORIGIN

Sukkot is a harvest celebration as well. In earlier times, it was celebrated in gratitude for the harvest that was collected. The huts resemble the constructions where the harvest used to be stored.

....

....

The palm branch (lulav) and etrog (a type of lemon) are important attributes of Sukkot. Both are used during religious ceremonies.

believers shake a little bouquet made from all of these, called the lulav, during the reading of the psalms. It is their way of asking God to take care of all nature.

Tourists need not feel left out when the Jews seek comfort in their sukkah. Snack bars, hotels and restaurants build their own, so everyone can camp out, or at least eat a meal, in one of the huts. And the little stands on the street that sell sukkah supplies and decorations - sleeping bags, roof materials and herbs – really bring the streets to life.

During the Sukkot week, observant Jews, who are not allowed to work during the celebration, hop enthusiastically from hut to hut to visit friends and family. Food is served everywhere and psalms are recited. The last day is Hoshana Rabba, when special services are held in the synagogues and the worshippers walk seven times around the place of worship. When all of this is done, the sukkah are dismantled and packed up again until next year.

Art Car Fest

SOME SAY THAT CLOTHES MAKE THE MAN. WELL, THAT'S NOT ENOUGH FOR ART CAR ENTHUSIASTS. YOUR CAR, THAT'S WHAT IT'S ALL ABOUT. *YOU ARE WHAT YOU DRIVE.* AND WHO WANTS TO BE A DULL, GREY STATION WAGON? BUT A STATION WAGON COVERED IN A THOUSAND LITTLE TIN SOLDIERS, PAINTED IN PICASSO STYLE OR TRANSFORMED INTO A GOTHIC CHURCH OR A PAIR OF RED PUMPS? NOW THAT'S SOMETHING TO GET EXCITED ABOUT.

UNITED STATES

The Bay Area, San Francisco, United States.

....

TIPS

If you're thinking of building one yourself, keep in mind that covering a fancy car with thousands of pens has already been done. Yup, that was the Mercedes Penz.

....

PARTICIPATE

Yes, of course! If you don't already have an art car, build one. That way, you can drive in the parade for free. If that's too much effort – or if you are stuck with a rental car – you can also be a volunteer. Volunteers can help with parking the cars, among other things. Check www.artcarfest.com for all the information.

....

It's not clear where the art car *movement* started. Perhaps it was inspired by John Lennon and Janis Joplin; he drove a hysterically painted Rolls Royce and she a psychedelic Porsche. At that time those cars seemed extreme, and on dull highways and in strip mall parking lots today, perhaps they still would be. But those vehicles wouldn't even get a second look at ArtCar Fest. During this festival, art car drivers congregate in San Francisco for four days to drive their pieces of art through the streets. Here you might catch a glimpse of a car transformed into a Mondrian-style work of art, even including the outfit of the female driver. There you can spot a Student Driver car, complete with a telephone pole piercing the side door and a leg with roller-skates dangling from the wheel. A car with female emancipation art, a car resembling a snail shell or a dinosaur – if you can imagine it, you will likely see it here.

The rule is that each art car must be street-legal. So it needs to be able to maintain a certain speed and cannot be too wide. The owners are easily able to work within these parameters to create astounding works of art. Thumbs of approval and friendly honking by strangers are all part of the experience, and the drivers clearly relish the attention. It is a creative hobby that comes with a riding gallery.

During ArtCar Fest, spectators are astonished by the creativity on display, and they even get the opportunity to talk with the motorists about their bizarre creations and their inspirations. The drivers make each other green with envy with the originality and ingenuity of their designs; one idea is more incredible than the next (a living garden on a car roof! Why didn't I think of that?!) They also swap technical information about, say, the best glue technique for sticking thousands of small pieces of plastic to your hood.

The festival also features a fashion show. Audience members are welcome to participate as long as they bring something funky to wear. That might be a wise thing to do anyway, since, after you've watched hundreds of art cars and their sparkling drivers pass by, you may just feel a bit boring when you step into your plain little Fiat at the end of the day.

Vegetarian Festival

88

SEP

EVERY YEAR DURING THE FIRST NINE DAYS OF THE NINTH MONTH OF THE CHINESE CALENDAR. USUALLY SEPTEMBER/OCTOBER.

 THAILAND

Phuket, Thailand.

 TIPS

During the festival, parades can be found at various locations throughout the city. The website **www. phuketvegetarian.com** has a schedule of the parades and where they are happening. The most important of these takes place at the Jui Tui temple in Phuket.

 ORIGIN

The Taoist worshippers in China do not consider self-inflicted pain necessary to please the gods, but the Taoists in Phuket have believed this for almost 150 years. Researchers believe that the ritual of pain was brought over from a similar festival that takes place during a certain Malaysian festival. The Chinese in Phuket claim that the tradition began when a theater group came to Phuket and became ill. In order to get on the good side of one of their gods, the people decided to atone for their sins by fasting for nine days and were afterwards miraculously healed.

Since **1463**

IMAGINE THE LARGEST BARBEQUE SKEWER YOU'VE EVER SEEN. NOW, CAREFULLY INSERT IT THROUGH YOUR LEFT CHEEK, EXITING THROUGH YOUR RIGHT CHEEK. NOW ADD TEN MORE. THOSE ALREADY A BIT NAUSEATED BY THE IDEA SHOULDN'T PAY TOO MUCH ATTENTION TO THE PIERCING RITUAL AT THE VEGETARIAN FESTIVAL.

During this ritual, you'll see men stick huge swords through the cheeks of other men, all without anesthesia. It's obviously easier instead to watch the fascinating procession of men stumbling down the street. It can seem, when watching this curious parade, that the men come uncomfortably close to the small altars placed on the streets, but it's actually all part of the festival. Store and home owners place these altars out on the streets in front of their houses and businesses for the participants. The Song Ma, as the religious devotees taking part in the ritual are called, take flowers, fruit or one of the nine cups of tea that sit ready on the small altars.

This festival, celebrated by the Chinese community in Phuket, honors the nine major gods of Taoism. The tradition requires that the Song Ma fast for a full month – that means no sex, no alcohol, and no meat. The festival occurs during the first nine days of abstinence. The self-induced pain they endure during the ritual, enhanced by the drums, dancing and fireworks, throws the Song Ma into a trance. Through this trance state, the Song Ma are believed to serve as mediums. It's clear that the spectators, with a combination of admiration, devotion and fear, consider the mediums who have pierced themselves to be blessed, and therefore offer them the fruit, flowers, and tea. But the festival also has a lighter side; stalls line the streets, colorfully-dressed children dance in and around the temples, and music fills the air as parades jam the streets and the city comes alive. And, of course, delicious fruit and vegetable dishes can be found everywhere.

Oktoberfest

THE MAYOR OF MUNICH, CLAD IN LEDERHOSEN, BEGINS THE FESTIVITIES AT TWELVE NOON BY TAPPING THE FIRST BARREL OF BEER. AND SO BEGINS OKTOBERFEST – SIXTEEN DAYS OF PURE DRINKING PLEASURE.

You can reassure yourself that you're not just drinking beer for days on end but are also learning many new things. Beer is part of the culture here in Bavaria, after all. And, if you start drinking at ten in the morning, you can learn so much about the different taste sensations of the six Munich beers on offer. That's so much more educational than a trip to a museum, isn't it?

Even outside the fourteen massive beer tents, there's a lot going on. There are fireworks, lots of music, and a dizzying array of attractions. On the first Sunday of Oktoberfest there is a big parade featuring people wearing traditional outfits. The organizers have made some adjustments to this ever-growing festival, which now attracts over six million visitors who drink millions of liters of beer. During the daytime, the music is a little softer – the big parties begin only later in the evening, after the elderly and the families with little kids have gone home. But don't worry – if you've been over-served and end up joining the ranks of the *bierleichen* (literally, "beer corpses"), there are brigades of first aid volunteers, usually eager young people, who will come to your aid. And if you're thinking of bringing your much-used beer mug (called a *Mass*) home from Oktoberfest with you, keep in mind that every year the guards at the exits fish out more than sixty thousand mugs from jacket pockets and handbags. At least try to think of a better hiding place for your souvenir.

89

OKT

SIXTEEN DAYS IN SEPTEMBER AND OCTOBER. THE LAST DAY FALLS ON THE FIRST SUNDAY OF OCTOBER.

 GERMANY

On the Theresienwiese site in Munich, Germany.

·····························

 **PARTICIPATE**

Drinking alone is not fully participating. If you're feeling really enthusiastic, rent or buy a Bavarian outfit: lederhosen for the guys or a dirndl for girls.

·····························

ANNO **ORIGIN**

The first Oktoberfest was held in 1810 to honor the wedding of Crown Prince Louis of Bavaria and Princess Therese of Saxe-Hildburghausen (hence the Theresienwiese, the main space where the festivities take place). The horse races that were part of the original festivities have been phased out over the years.

·····························

TIPS

Book a seat at a table ahead of time. For more info, visit **www.oktoberfest.de**. If you haven't booked ahead, show up early in the day. The tents are open weekdays for ten hours and for nine hours during the weekend. Each tent has its own character. All the details can be found online, so just check the website for more information and to book. Take along enough cash, since you won't get too far with only a credit or debit card.

·····························

GERMANY

BERLIN

Lost during the
Oktoberfest 2010:
• 1.450 pieces of clothes
• 770 ID cards
• 420 wallets
• 37 children
• 1 live rabbit

MUNICH

Gorilla Run

SEVEN KILOMETERS. IT'S EASY ENOUGH TO WALK THAT DISTANCE, IN FLIP-FLOPS, WITH NO TRAINING WHATSOEVER. IT'S THE MANDATORY HAIRY GORILLA SUIT THAT TURNS THIS INTO AN EXHAUSTING TASK. ESPECIALLY IF YOU ARE DETERMINED TO KEEP THE HEAT-TRAPPING FACE MASK WITH TINY EYE HOLES INTACT.

On the route that runs along the Thames River, passing the Tate Modern and the Tower Bridge, there is also a massive stairwell. It's easy to miss a step since it's so hard to see out of your mask. In the instructions that the organization sends along with your gorilla costume, they include this tip: practice with your suit on. That's the only way you will notice that the legs of the suit are way too long and the eye holes likely too small. Nip and tuck that thing! You want to make sure that your suit is as perfect as can be before the start of the annual Gorilla Run in London.

At the start of the race, the organizers hand out headbands that will help keep your gorilla mask from wobbling too much and obstructing your view. The purpose of this sportsmanlike costume event is the preservation of the gorilla. Everyone who signs up for the run pays eighty pounds and promises to collect at least four hundred pounds in donations. For your registration money, you get a fundraising pack, a gorilla suit, as well as those handy instructions mentioned earlier. On top of that, you get your own fundraising website so that your friends, acquaintances and colleagues can donate money to the organization and you can keep close track of who loves you (and the apes).

The Gorilla Organization primarily donates the collected money – a couple thousand pounds per year –to the people living near the gorillas' habitat, the African rainforest. The hope is to provide these poor people with alternative means of supporting themselves other than mining, farming, hunting and thereby damaging the gorillas' habitat. The pounds that you raise by sweating it out in that suit are also provided to schools in villages close to the territory of the endangered apes.

But there's more to it than just donning a suit and running. The British like to do things over the top. Not only are you dressed up as a gorilla, you *are* a gorilla. And since this is a fun run, the gorillas wear costumes. Previously spotted along the race route: a gorilla dressed up as a banana, gorillas in tutus, gorillas dressed as marathon runners, a gorilla as a boxer, one as bikini model, and a bunch of gorillas dressed up as a native African tribe, complete with raffia skirts, coconut bikinis, the works. You can try to do even better than that.

90

ENGLAND

London, England

⚡ **PARTICIPATE**

Definitely! About seven hundred people participate in the sponsor run and the organization hopes to see that number increase. You can sign up through the website www.greatgorillas. org. The cost is £80. You will get the gorilla suit sent to you at home.

ANNO **ORIGIN**

The first gorilla run was held in 2003.

👍 **TIPS**

⚡ The suits are quite large, so don't overestimate your size when you fill out the form.
⚡ If the sweat starts streaming right through your saturated eyebrows, take off your mask.
⚡ This is not a speed contest; there are also prizes for the best-dressed gorillas.

TICKETS

The cost for the people around you will be at least be £400, all in donations. It's also fine to walk.

the gorilla organization **START**

Les Batailles de Reines

Since 1923

SO YOU THINK GIRLS CAN'T FIGHT? GO TAKE A LOOK AT THE COW FIGHTS TAKING PLACE IN THE VALAIS REGION OF SWITZERLAND AND HAVE YOUR MIND CHANGED. UP HERE IN THIS PART OF THE ALPS, THE STRONGEST COWS LOCK HORNS TO DETERMINE WHO WILL BE THE ALPHA FEMALE OF THE GROUP. AND THE SWISS PEOPLE LOVE IT.

All those Alps chocolate commercials would have you believe that everything is so peaceful and happy up in the mountains. That is simply not the case, since, as soon as these ladies leave their winter stables every year, a massive fight breaks out. Who will be in charge of the group this year? The local Eringer cows (or Hérens) are super-combative. They are small and muscular, blessed with wide foreheads that serve both as their weapons and their cushions.

As soon as a cow has identified her opponent, and both are willing to fight, the two put their foreheads together, clamp horns, and begin pushing at full force. It is all about pushing the other one back, or down, until the weaker one forfeits, leaving a hoof mark in the grass.

91

🌐 **SWITZERLAND**

In the canton of Valais, with the finale in Martigny, Switzerland.

Starting in the 1920s, the Swiss turned the cows' natural fighting behavior into a local amusement that lasts for many months. There are various qualifying rounds and, by the time winter is almost in sight, a finale. All farmers with Erdinger cows in the region of Valais are able to participate in the competition. They let their strongest milk producers combat in the qualifications, which are organized in different pastures.

The girls all get a number painted on their sides and are gathered by weight class in the meadow. Any cow that doesn't feel like fighting and turns away from the group is taken off the battleground by men, using sticks. The cows must feel like brawling themselves; they are not forced to do so. On some days, there is not much happening, but on others there are several battles going on at the same time and the clanging of cow bells fills the air. The cows fume and fret, stamp their hooves, and prepare for battle. The losing ladies are taken off the field as they are defeated, until one proud winner, *la reine*, is the only one left.

The real showdown happens in October, when the best of the best are gathered in the Roman amphitheater in Martigny. Thousands of people buy tickets to witness La Bataille de Reines and to witness who will be crowned *La Reine des Reines*, the queen of the queens, at the end of the day. It's a big day not only for the winner herself but also for her owner. Not only because the farmer and cow are so close that the farmers often spoil their best cows with wine and cake, but also because the value of the future calves of the queen will have just risen substantially in value. As a reward, the queen must get a fancy spot in the winter stable.

Angola Rodeo

BUYING A FRIED CHICKEN WING FROM A MURDERER, OR PERHAPS A PAINTING FROM A RAPIST. WITNESSING HOW MEN WHO HAVE BEEN CONVICTED FOR LIFE TRY TO RIDE A BULL. AS STRANGE AS IT MAY SEEM, A DAY OUT FOR TOURISTS AND CONVICTS AT THE SAME TIME IS WHAT THE ANGOLA PRISON PROUDLY PROMOTES.

The spectacle can't help but remind one a bit of one of the more unseemly aspects of ancient Rome, when slaves and prisoners battled lions in the Coliseum in front of thousands of cheering spectators. But most of the "gladiators" of the Angola prison have never ridden a horse before, let alone seen a bull from up close, and there is no practice allowed. It's simply put on your clothes and head out into the arena. Professional rodeo clowns are in the ring to distract the enraged bulls whenever a convict is really struggling. Not even this prison is going to risk bad publicity.

Angola, another name for the Louisiana State Penitentiary, is the biggest state prison in America, with over five thousand inmates. Before it held a prison, the piece of land was a cotton plantation that was worked by slaves. Now the hard work is done by the prison's long term residents, about three quarters of whom are serving a life sentence. The rodeo is a welcome distraction from prison life. The fight with the bull offers the prisoners six seconds of freedom - no one tells them what to do, no one determines how they handle the situation. Those six seconds are about nothing more than each

UNITED STATES

Angola Prison, 35 km northeast of St. Francisville, Louisiana, United States.

TICKETS

At $15, for sale at **www.angolarodeo.com**.

DICTIONARY

Bull Riding: One of the most dangerous parts of the rodeo. The inexperienced convict sits on a massive bull. For a chance at the title of 'all round cowboy' he must stay on the bull for six seconds.

Convict Poker: Four inmates are playing poker in the arena. Suddenly one of the fences opens up and a raging bull runs towards them. The last man still sitting is the winner.

Guts & Glory: The fiercest bull has a poker chip bound around his neck. The man who can get the chip wins first.

ORIGIN

The first Angola Rodeo was held in 1965, for fun, just for prisoners and coworkers. Two years later, a couple of people from the outside were allowed to watch, and another two years after that a stadium for 4.500 people was built. A market was later added to the rodeo, and in 2000 the new stadium for ten thousand people was opened.

man's determination, courage, and skill. The prison emphasizes that every inmate voluntarily participates in the rodeo and that the money raised from it is spent on noble causes, like a new chapel or new material for the recreation room. The stadium where the rodeo takes place, which can hold up to six thousand spectators, was built by inmates.

Only convicted criminals with top marks for behavior can participate in the rodeo. Yet, despite that fact, it can nevertheless be a bit bizarre to stroll around a market place where you know that almost everyone wearing a jumpsuit has likely done something horrible. The quaint names of the various groups selling food and other items can seem a bit incongruous with the whole maximum security prison situation. The Methodist Men's Fellowship sells chicken, the Full Gospel Fellowship has shrimp, and the AA group roasted potatoes. You can get your picture taken as a prisoner, by a prisoner. At the arts and crafts market, inmates sell wood carvings, assembled miniature ships and paintings, inspired by their lives before Angola. Perhaps the best pieces of art come from suffering.

92

Ghadames festival

93

THE CENTURIES-OLD DESERT VILLAGE OF GHADAMES HAS BEEN ABANDONED SINCE THE 1980s. ONLY DURING THE THREE-DAY FESTIVAL DO THE FORMER INHABITANTS RETURN TO THEIR BEAUTIFUL OLD MUD HOUSES. THEY GATHER TO CELEBRATE WEDDINGS, TO HOST FAMILY PARTIES AND, ON OCCASION, TO ENTERTAIN THE TOURISTS A BIT.

At some point, someone will realize that money can be made from this unique celebration in such a stunning location. But the Libyans don't seem to have figured this out yet; the festival has neither a website nor a distinct schedule. This lack of sophistication gives the festival a special feeling; as you can feel that you've been allowed a peek into the private desert world of the locals.

The Ghadames festival celebrates desert culture in all its forms and for every social group. It is usually celebrated in October, when the dates are ripe and the men climb into the trees around the oasis to pick them. For centuries, this has been the time of the year when everyone from the surrounding regions gathers to celebrate the harvest and to trade. The desert nomads come to tell their stories, to dance, to let others enjoy their music, and to organize camel races. Market vendors come from all over Libya to sell their goods, and the people of Ghadames come out in force to proudly celebrate their culture. They do this not only with singing and dancing, but also by showing off their old houses, which the government forced them to abandon for the more modern town a bit further away, as the crumbling desert structures were deemed too dangerous to inhabit.

For some families, the festival provides the opportunity to return to their old homes to host family parties, to get engaged, or to negotiate marriages. The most important attraction is the old town of Ghadames, 'the jewel of the Sahara', which is a UNESCO World Heritage site. The narrow, winding streets of mud houses form a labyrinth. Some of the alleyways are covered; in others you can see up to the clear blue sky and feel the burning sun. Just as in a village made of Legos, all the parts are connected. The outside of all the homes is white, but this uniform exterior belies the bright colors to be found inside.

During the festival, you can hear music blowing through the old village and you can see little children running barefoot through the dusty streets, stopping every now and then to stare at the tourists. During the festivities, the Touaregs make their camp nearby, at an oasis in the desert. After you have ridden a camel with them, danced to their music, and embraced their mysteriously elegant desert look with a turban, you can even sand board down the dunes. Don't forget to climb back up to the top of the dunes, though, to see how the sunset colors the gleaming sand; keep watching until the only sparkles you see are the ones coming from the stars.

🌍 LIBYA

Ghadames, Libya

👍 TIPS

Only minimal information about the festival is available, but you can find some on the website **www.temehu.com.**

⚡ PARTICIPATE

Get ready to watch the sunset, take a ride on a camel, congratulate newlyweds, dance with the Touaregs, and eat tons and tons of dates.

Diwali

THOUSANDS OF LIGHTS ILLUMINATE THE SIKHS AND REFLECT OFF THE HOLY WATER IN THEIR MOST FAMOUS PLACE OF WORSHIP, THE HARMANDIR SAHIB TEMPLE. DIWALI, THE FESTIVAL OF LIGHTS, IS CELEBRATED BY INDIANS OF ALL FAITHS, ALTHOUGH THE DIFFERENT FAITHS HAVE THEIR OWN GODS AND UNIQUE DIWALI TRADITIONS.

KAR

ANNUALLY ON THE 15TH DAY OF THE HINDU MONTH OF KARTIKA (USUALLY OCTOBER OR NOVEMBER).

🌐 INDIA

In the Harmandir Sahib temple in Amristar, Punjab, India

....

....

👍 TIPS

Amristar is packed during Diwali, so be sure to make your accommodation arrangements well in advance. Otherwise, you'll surely need divine intervention to get a decent place to stay.

....

⚡ PARTICIPATE

Sikhs allow anyone into the sanctuaries, but you will need to follow a specific set of rules: No eating meat, no drinking and no smoking. You will also need head coverings (men included). Make sure to take your shoes off and to wash your feet at the entrance.

....

94

The Hindus keep themselves busy with the wanderings of Rama and with lights to lure Lakshmi, the goddess of wealth, into their homes. Rama carries a stick with him to drive away poverty. Hindus celebrate Diwali mainly as a family celebration, so cozy nights at home along with many lit candles and bowls of food are common. The Sikhs celebrate Diwali through the various heroic exploits and struggles of their many gurus. The main celebration, where all Sikhs aspire to be, takes place at the Harmandir Sahib, or the golden temple, located in northern India. One of the stories that is honored is that of the sixth guru, Guru Hargobind Ji, who was released from prison in 1619. Through an incredibly ingenious trick, he also managed to set free 52 other princes that were held captive. The Sikhs celebrated this by lighting candles at their then-new temple, and they have continued to do so for centuries. Throughout the day and night, visiting Hindus come and go through the spacious, well-lit halls of the Harmandir Sahib. The worshippers light oil lamps, sing, and walk along the promenades of the temple, honoring their gurus and losing themselves in the enchanting flickering of the burning candles. Sikhs come from all over the world to walk around the sacred pool of immortality, while fireworks explode overhead, revealing the magnificent golden roof of the temple.

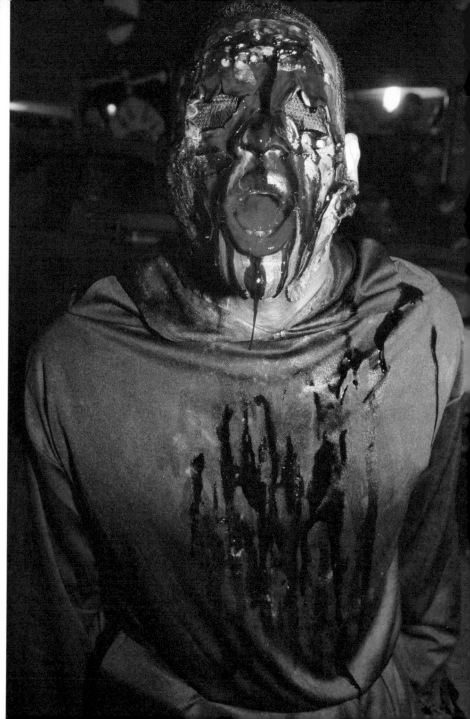

Halloween

TENS OF THOUSANDS OF FLAMBOYANT ARTISTS, ACTORS, DANCERS AND OTHER CREATIVE CHARACTERS – IN COSTUMES BEYOND BELIEF – COME OUT IN FORCE ONCE A YEAR FOR THE GREENWICH VILLAGE HALLOWEEN PARADE. AMERICA'S LARGEST HALLOWEEN CELEBRATION, THIS IS ONE OF NEW YORK'S MOST OUTRAGEOUS EVENTS.

 UNITED STATES

Greenwich Village, New York, along 6th Avenue.

⚡ **PARTICIPATE**

Any person can join if he or she is dressed for it. It takes at least two hours for the entire parade to go by, so if you arrive a bit late, there is still plenty of time to catch some of the action. If you don't have the time or the inclination to make a costume, you can also register as a volunteer to help carry one of the large, specially-built puppets. See more at **www.halloween-nyc.com**.

ORIGIN

Halloween likely originated with the Celtic festival Samhain, which marked the end of the season of light and heralded the coming season of darkness. The Celts believed that the border between this world and the other world faded on Samhain and that spirits could cross back over to the world of the living. Ancestors were honored and invited back, but people hoped to scare off the evil spirits with scary scenes.

While admiring the over-the-top costumes and taking in this astonishing sight, you might just forget that Halloween in America is totally commercialized. For the Halloween Parade, a participant can't just show up in one of the countless ready-made costumes that go on sale months in advance in stores throughout the city. The celebrants create their own highly imaginative, and sometimes scandalous, disguises. You might see beautifully crafted giant dolls, illuminated floats, or perhaps a group of people portraying a full deck of cards or a bunch of Scrabble letters (likely formed into dirty words).

The Halloween Parade began in 1973 when a local mask maker and puppeteer got his friends and their children together to wear masks and head out onto the neighborhood streets. From those beginnings, the parade has exploded in popularity and now draws a few million spectators every year in addition to the 50.000 participants. The distinction between participants and spectators is also not clear cut, since many viewers along the route are often in costumes and can be tempted to step off the sidewalk to join the masses.

Dozens of bands perform, traveling either on floats or on foot. Some groups of friends bring their own speakers with them because music is part of their costume – a bunch of skeletons might keep blasting Thriller, for example. Needless to say, the end of the parade does not mean the end of the festivities – the revelers disperse all over the city to various bars, clubs, and, of course, costume parties.

95

Dia del Gaucho

CHASING THE COWS ALL BY YOURSELF. JUST YOU, YOUR HORSE, YOUR KNIFE, THE OPEN PLAINS, AND NO ONE TO BOTHER YOU. LIGHTING A FIRE AT NIGHT TO SLOWLY ROAST A JUICY PIECE OF MEAT. AGRIBUSINESS MAY BE RENDERING MORE AND MORE GAUCHOS OBSOLETE, BUT THE ARGENTINIAN COWBOY CULTURE IS STILL CELEBRATED EVERY YEAR.

Those legendary chunks of red juiciness, the dripping Angus your teeth slides through as though it were butter... that's the gaucho culture distilled to its purest form. The Argentinian cowboy lets his cattle roam for miles to find enough grass to fill their four stomachs, since this results in the tastiest meat. He roasts the steaks slowly over an open fire – *asado* is the name of this roasting technique that has become world famous. But alas, modern times have not been too kind to the gauchos. They still exist, but large sections of the pampas have been taken over for agricultural use. Many Argentinian cattle live in the same miserable circumstances as livestock elsewhere in the world; they are fattened up as fast as possible in small sheds. And the gauchos have largely abandoned their lifestyle to become employees in factories for low wages.

96

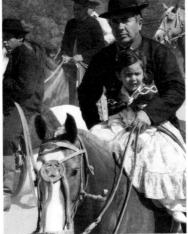

🌐 **ARGENTINA**

San Antonio de Areco, Argentina

⚡ **PARTICIPATE**

There are plenty of possibilities to pretend you're a gaucho for a day or longer. In San Antonio de Areco, you can arrange horseback riding journeys, ranging from one hour to a couple of days. Ponchos are included, for those who are so inclined.

👍 **TIPS**

Check **www.sanantonio-deareco.com** for dates and more detailed schedule. In case of bad weather, the Dia del Gaucho is postponed a week.

Even though thousands of gauchos now must work regular day jobs, they lead the rest of their lives on horseback and try to uphold their proud traditions. Once a year, gauchos from all of northern Argentina gather in the little town of San Antonio de Areco, just northwest of Buenos Aires. Some of the men make the four day journey on horseback, or in a carriage pulled by a horse, just to be there. The Dia del Gaucho falls within the weeklong celebration of La Fiesta de la Tradición. Throughout the week, there are exhibitions, local bands performing, and lots of souvenirs for sale. But the real party begins on cowboy day. Hundreds of horses march through the streets, carrying the stately gauchos clad in their most beautiful ponchos, with their *facón* (long knife) tucked in their belts behind their backs. The women ride wearing their finest dresses, the skirts draped over their horses.

There are rodeos taking place on the big field, as well as horse sprints and other games involving horses. And, naturally, there is lots of delicious food. The whole town smells like barbecue. As the steaks are slowly cooking, the gauchos dance their traditional dances and the ladies dance elegantly in the dusty streets, all to the melancholy music of the troubadours. An element of melancholy is only appropriate, since life for the gauchos hasn't been easy. But no one is thinking about that on this festive day. Fiesta!

Día de los Muertos

MEXICO

Oaxaca (and the rest of Mexico).

PARTICIPATE

You do not need to have a family tomb in Mexico to enjoy the festivities. In Oaxaca, join one of the street parties, in costume or not. Walking at night in one of the cemeteries will provide you with another glimpse into the celebration, and you might even be invited to do a shot of tequila in honor of the dead.

ORIGIN

The Aztecs celebrated the temporary non-physical return of the souls for a month, around August. In an effort to sell more native people on Catholicism, the Spaniards married the traditional beliefs to Christian ones and this celebration became All Saints' Day.

97

TEQUILA, CHICKEN LEGS, MARIACHI BANDS, DRESSING UP, AND DANCING NEXT TO YOUR LOVED ONES' GRAVES... DURING DÍA DE LOS MUERTOS IN MEXICO, CEMETERIES ARE THE PLACE TO PARTY.

On November 1, Dia de los Angelitos, it's the deceased children who are remembered, and on November 2, Dia de los Muertos, it's the adults. Rather than spending the day in mourning, the Mexicans celebrate. The Aztecs believed that departed souls occasionally return, and that this happens during the day. So, naturally, it would be a sin to waste those precious moments together in tears.

Preparations for the day begin weeks in advance. Coffins made from sugar, marzipan, and chocolate line the shelves, and shop windows are filled with skeleton figures in costume, dancing, riding bikes, or just doing everyday things. In their homes, families build altars overflowing with bread, fruit, candy, candles, and decorations to welcome back their lost loved ones. Also standard on the altar: a bowl of water so that the spirit can quench his thirst after the long journey. The arch made of yellow marigolds on the altar is the portal that allows the souls to re-enter our world.

The day is celebrated throughout Mexico, but the biggest celebration is in the south of the country, where the culture of the indigenous people still flourishes. In the small city of Oaxaca, there are processions of cheerful skeletons through the streets as well as major public street parties with live music and dancing "dead" people. During the day, many families clean the graves of their dead relatives and decorate them for the upcoming evening party. They place many candles on the picnic blanket next to the grave, they put the relative's favorite beverage on the tombstone, and then the marching band comes along and everyone parties. As a visitor, you can just soak up the atmosphere and enjoy the parties with the families. Chances are you'll also be invited to have a drink with some new Mexican friends – and also the spirits of their relatives, of course.

Loy Krathong

NAILS, HAIR, FLAKES OF SKIN... PUT THEM ALL INTO A FLOATING KRATHONG, PUSH IT INTO THE WATER, AND THEN YOU WILL BE RELIEVED OF THE THINGS YOU DON'T LIKE ABOUT YOURSELF. AND THE COMING YEARS WILL ALL BE BETTER. LOY KRATHONG IS A THAI FESTIVAL ABOUT GIVING THANKS FOR THE RAINY SEASON AND CELEBRATING THE RICE HARVEST. BUT IT'S ALSO A TIME TO REFLECT AND TO PRAY FOR A SPEEDY RESOLUTION TO YOUR PROBLEMS.

98

NOV

ON THE DAY OF THE FULL MOON IN THE TWELFTH LUNAR MONTH, USUALLY IN NOVEMBER.

 THAILAND

Chiang Mai (and the rest of Thailand).

ORIGIN

Scholars still argue about the true origin of the festival, although the prevailing legend is the one of Nang Noppamas, the daughter of a Brahmin priest. About seven hundred years ago, she wanted to thank the goddess of water. She fashioned a bowl of leaves into the shape of a lotus flower and sent it out to the water goddess filled with incense and a candle - the first krathong.

 PARTICIPATE

In the morning, send your krathong out into the water, loaded with all the terrible qualities about yourself from which you want to be freed. In the evening, release a beautiful lantern into the sky for good luck.

Loy means "to float" and a *krathong* is a container traditionally made from banana leaves. Everyone places an offering into a krathong: incense, lotus flowers, a candle, or a small amount of money. Some people also place their own nails into their krathongs as a symbol of the evil in themselves. The krathongs are then pushed out into the water and the participants' troubles sail away with them. Couples often push their offerings out into the water together; it's said that they can get insight into the future of their relationship by seeing whether their krathongs float together or drift apart.

While the festival is celebrated throughout Thailand, it's most beautiful in Chiang Mai, where both banks of the river are exquisitely decorated. Once the sun sets behind the rolling hills of the city, everyone gets excited about start of the parades and the fireworks. Sponsored light-covered floats go by and Thai beauties roam the city, while others perform traditional dances to the sounds of drum bands. The highlight for everyone is the launching of the *Khom Fai* (or Khoom Loy) lanterns into the sky. The sight of thousands of them filling the dark void is truly extraordinary. Each Thai person keeps track of his own lantern as it floats up into the sky, until it disappears into the beautiful mass of lights.

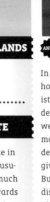

🌐 CAYMAN ISLANDS

Grand Cayman,
Cayman Islands.

⚡ PARTICIPATE

Dress up! To participate in
the competitions, you usually have to pay, and much
of the money goes towards
community service projects.
See **www.piratesweekfesti-
val.com**.

📅 ORIGIN

In 1977, Grand Cayman was
hoping to attract more tourists. So the tourism board
decided that what tourists
were seeking, naturally, was
more entertainment. They
decided on the pirate theme,
given the island's heritage.
But this was all to the great
dissatisfaction of the devout
Christian community on the
island who believed that the
island's youth were being
led astray during these
eleven days of partying.

Pirates Week

A GREAT TRADITION DOES NOT NECESSARILY HAVE TO MAKE SENSE. PIRATES WEEK ON THE ISLAND OF GRAND CAYMAN NOT ONLY LASTS LONGER THAN ONE WEEK, BUT IS ALSO NOT REALLY HISTORICALLY ACCURATE. REGARDLESS, THE THOUSANDS OF VISITORS WHO FLOCK TO THIS BEAUTIFUL ISLAND FOR THE FESTIVAL DON'T SEEM TO MIND THE INCONSISTENCIES.

The story goes that the island was once the base for the most dangerous pirates prowling the oceans. For many, the highlight of the eleven-day festival is the mock pirate invasion. Two old ships come "suddenly" into George Town harbor, unloading a number of angry pirates onto the pier, where thousands of people -often in pirate get-ups themselves- tremble with fear. The invasion is never the same - every year a new twist is added (water canons, fire, or additional floating surprises) to keep things interesting. Throughout the festival, the whole city is abuzz with activity: parades, fireworks, lots of beer drinking and dancing to Caribbean music. And occasionally a spontaneous sword fight breaks out, since acting the part of the pirate is much more fun after a few strong rum cocktails. The organization also makes sure that the celebration contains some competitive elements. These include pirate running races (complete with wooden legs), a costume contest, a serious karaoke show and the challenging Underwater Treasure Hunt. This contest – again, pirate attire is appreciated – involves collecting as many coins as possible from an underwater reef. You can compete with full scuba or snorkeling gear, but the really tough Captain Jack Sparrows among the treasure hunters just dive in without any modern equipment, swords in hand, parrots on their shoulders.

99

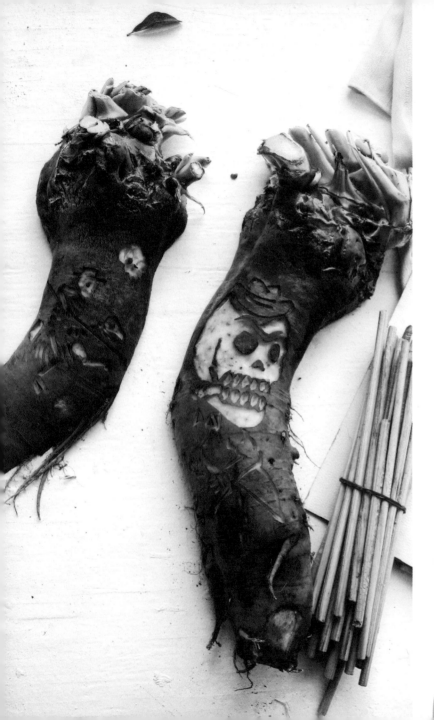

Noche de los Rabanos

PERHAPS YOU'VE SEEN LOTUS FLOWERS USED AS DECORATION IN CHINESE RESTAURANTS? MEXICANS ALSO KNOW A LITTLE SOMETHING ABOUT MAKING WORKS OF ART FROM PLANTS AND VEGETABLES. DURING THE NOCHE DE LOS RABANOS IN OAXACA, RADISHES ARE CARVED INTO THE MOST EXQUISITE AND MIND-BOGGLING CREATIONS.

Humble little radishes will not suffice for this vegetable-carving extravaganza right before Christmas. The artisans work with huge, specially grown radishes. These can be over a foot long and can weigh as much as three pounds each. The variety of figures into which these radishes are sculpted is staggering, as is the skill with which the figures are rendered. You might radishes chiseled into animals, a bunch of flowers, a nativity scene, a celebrity, or a dancer wearing a delicate lace dress.

Some artists find working with radishes too restrictive and instead make designs from dried corn husks and dried flower petals. These artisans can now

100

enter the competition, too. The color that these new creations add to the exhibition can – after viewing so many radish figures - come as a bit of welcome relief.

On the morning of December 23rd, Oaxaca's famed *zocolo* begins to buzz with activity. There's a children's workshop, for the budding radish carvers of the next generation. Then the artisans arrive and set up their perfectly-arranged displays. The event lasts seven hours, during which the square is packed with thousands of people admiring and photographing the imaginative works of art. The audience strolls from stand to stand, under a dark sky illuminated by Christmas lights. The winner of the competition earns about one thousand US dollars, plus a coveted photo placement on the front page of the next day's local newspaper. After the winner is announced, there are fireworks and music. While the artisans take apart their stands, the crowds head to the restaurants and pubs. And if admiring all these vegetable master-pieces has given you the urge to buy something beautiful, you can always head to the cathedral, where a night market stands ready to welcome all customers.

 TIPS

↯ Make sure not to take a bite out of one of the radish artworks or out of the large radishes that are waiting to be carved. These are harvested two weeks later than usual, and they are grown with a host of chemicals to make them so gigantic.

↯ The following day there is a parade made up of lots of floats in the center of Oaxaca. Local churches are also worth visiting at this time of year, since they are filled with pageants and beautiful decorations.

🌐 **MEXICO**

Oaxaca, Mexico.

⚜ **ORIGIN**

The Spanish brought radishes to Mexico in the 16th century. In the 19th century, it's believed that market vendors started crafting their radishes into interesting shapes and scenes to appeal to the shopping housewives. This proved to be a great success and women began buying the sculptures to decorate their holiday tables. In 1897, the mayor of Oaxaca launched the first of the now-famous exhibitions in the city's main square.

PHOTO CREDITS

27. Valencia Tourism, Yazmin Rosete
28. Sean
29. Dorin Nicolaescu-Musteata, Villem Alango
30. Hay Haenen, Douglas Sandoval
31. Flioukas Apostolis, Emmanouil Papadopoulos
32. Eddy Y. L. Chang
33. Ryan Buterbaugh, Mark Bajek
34. Khmanglo, Daniel Grosvenor
35. Paul Stein, Rona House
36. Mark Chipps, Irvine Short
37. Gregor Schnuer, Jonathan Carroll
38. Ron Rademaker, David Vermeulen
39. Stuart Wainstock
40. Wilda Fong, Victor Lam
41. Arnd Zschocke
42. Michal Czajkowsk
43. Simon Phillips
44. Mike Warren
45. Santidd
46. Totallydorset.wordpress.com
47. Kristen Micek
48. Michael Hartmann, *artist:* Lorie Hamel &
    Julie Fusilier *www.bodypainting-festival.com*,
    Michael Genswaider, *artist:* Lorie Hamel &
    Julie Fusilier *www.bodypainting-festival.com*,
    Katharina Kamitz, *artist:* John Vargas
    www.bodypainting-festival.com,
    Ulf Scherling, *artist:* Mylene Ruaux
    www.bodypainting-festival.com

49. Oscar Galvan
50. Maurizio Rufino, Alessandro Morandi
51. Nathan Pana
52. Joan R. Bellido
53. Hans Hendriksen, José Santana
54. Mike
55. Patricia Bruno, David 'DJ' Cloninger
56. Antonio Naranjo, Enrico Porcari
57. Tonya Peterson, City of Roswell, Noel Brewer
58. Martin Brawley, José Fco Parra García
59. Hannu Keranen
60. Dave Douglass
61. Chuck Coker, Abigail Beronich
62. Len Payne
63. Ashley Lightfoot, Michael Gordon
64. Dan Treadwell.
65. Dana Astmann
66. David Bueno Gutierrez
67. Andy Newman/Florida Keys News Bureau/HO
68. Alberto Varela
69. Andrew Clelland
70. Massimiliano De Giorgi
71. Ramon Stoppelenburg
72. Jean Claude Labe, Martin Stabenfeldt
73. Bashar Shglila, Bill Garnett
74. Frida Nyberg, Umberto Luparelli
75. Maison du Tourisme van Dinant
76. Mike Houghton
77. Owen Foreman, Helen Beck

78. Katrine Syppli Kohl, Marilee
79. Fotograferen.net
80. Dmitry
81. Jeff Eloy
82. Andy Tree, Mario Groleau
83. Luigi P. Carta
84. James Addison, Miriam van Oort
85. Xavier Miralles Martinez
86. Yaniv Yaakubovich
87. Paul McRae, Simon Carless, Tom LaFaver
88. Michiel Souren
89. Bart Lapers
90. The Gorilla Organization: *www.gorillas.org*,
    David Vermeulen
91. Angelo Amboldi
92. Louisiana State Penitentiary, William Warner
93. Ibrahem Azaga, Bashar Shglila
94. Jagmeet Singh Hanspal, Gerald C. Menon
95. Leonard Rosmarin, Olivier Perrin
96. Eduardo Amorim, Olivier Graille
97. Paul Davis
98. Jeff Henig, Hans Hendriksen
99. John Allman Dayrit, Liz McGee,
    Joseph Domingo
100. Nick Turner, Tom LaFaver, Hans Proppe

Lightning Publishing Limited
© Lightning Publishing Ltd 2011
info@lightning-publishing.com
Hartfield Place
40-44 High Street
Northwood, Middlesex,
HA6 1BN
Great Britain

Text: Liedefix Imperium (Liedewij Loorbach), *www.liedefiximperium.com*
Art Direction: Studio Pino (David Pino & Stefan Altenburger), *www.studiopino.nl*
Icon design: Dutch Icon (Hemmo de Jonge), *www.dutchicon.com*
Copy editor: Amir Andriesse, *www.rbaa.nl*
Translation: Susie van den Berg
Print advice: Mediadam (Patrick Werkman)
Publisher: Lightning Publishing Limited
Research: Liedewij Loorbach, David Vermeulen
Photo cover: Roy Sullivan, National Park Service
Photo back cover: James Addison, Dmitry, Angelo Greco, Michiel Souren
ISBN: 978-0-9568059-2-8

Follow Sullivan's List online
www.facebook.com/sullivanslist
www.twitter.com/sullivanslist

Get Sullivan's List on your iPad

Get inspired and share your own experiences, tips, and photos at www.sullivanslist.com

 **PIFWORLD**
We dream. We donate. We act.

Not everybody can travel the world and attend the events that are on Sullivan's List. For that reason Sullivan's List supports the charity organization Pifworld. If you want to help as well please visit: www.pifworld.com

Sufficiently inspired and ready to pack your bags? Great! But do realize
when participating in foreign traditions and festivals that you are a guest.
Please respect the local communities and their customs.
Have a safe journey.